WHAT TO DO WHEN YOUR DOG . . .

DROOLS

Some canine breeds are more prone to drooling than others, and some simply drool in response to a pleasant stimulus, like the smell of food or being petted. It's best to take him to a vet to rule out any oral problem or infectious disease. If he drools in response to the smell of food cooking, try to feed him before you prepare your own food. If he's simply a drool-prone dog, keep a cloth handy to clean up his harmless habit.

INCESSANTLY LICKS, SCRATCHES, OR BITES HERSELF

First check to see if she's dirty or if she appears to have fleas, lice or other parasites living in her coat—either way bathing her in a veterinarian-approved flea and tick shampoo should do the trick. Certain skin disorders could also cause your pooch to itch, or, she could develop "lick sores" from too much licking due to stress. If you can figure out what it is, you could try to remove the offending stressor—but any skin problem that doesn't heal should be checked out by a veterinarian.

EXHIBITS ANTISOCIAL BEHAVIOR

If your dog shies away from other humans, don't force him to interact with people. Instead, guide him along by showing him that you don't fear the visitor—let him approach the person in his own time. You can also try having the visitor place a treat on the floor near where he or she is sitting, so the dog will eventually come over and eat it. Keep in mind that most antisocial dogs eventually overcome their shyness out of necessity.

FIND OUT OTHER WAYS TO CORRECT
BOTHERSOME DOG BEHAVIORS IN
BAD DOG!

St. Martin's Paperbacks Titles
by Steve Duno

NO, KITTY!
BAD DOG!

BAD DOG!

A Complete A–Z
Guide for When
Your Dog
Misbehaves

STEVE DUNO

St. Martin's Paperbacks

BAD DOG!

ISBN: 0-312-97582-1

Printed in the United States of America

St. Martin's Paperbacks edition / November 2000

10 9 8 7 6 5 4 3 2 1

CONTENTS

INTRODUCTION   1

PART ONE
The Dog: What You Need to Know First   5

PART TWO
Dog Behavior Problems, A–Z
   Aggression   36
   Antisocial Behavior   61
   Bad Breath   64
   Barking   65
   Bathing, Aversion To   73
   Begging   76
   Car Sickness   78
   Chasing   81
   Chewing   85
   Children, Intolerance Of   87
   Coprophagy, or Stool Eating   91
   Crate, Aversion To   93
   Crotch Sniffing   98
   Depression   100
   Destructive Behavior   104
   Digging   108
   Drinking from the Toilet   108
   Drooling   109
   Eating Toxic Substances and Objects   111
   Escaping   115
   Excessive Prey Drive   119
   Finicky Eating   123
   Flatulence   125

Garbage or Cupboard Raiding   127
Grooming and Handling, Aversion To   129
Hiding   134
House-soiling Problems   137
Humping   144
Ignoring Commands   146
Incessant Licking, Scratching, or Biting   149
Jumping on People and Furniture   152
Keep-away and Stealing   156
Mouthing or Biting   160
Old Age, Behavior Problems Related To   164
Overactive Behavior   167
Overeating   170
Pill Taking, Aversion To   173
Plant Eating   176
Pulling While on the Leash   179
Pushy or Rude Behavior   181
Running Away   185
Separation Anxiety   188
Sexual Problems   194
Swimming, Aversion To   196
Underactive Behavior   198
Veterinarian, Aversion To   199

PART THREE
The Ten Most Important Ways to Minimize
Canine Behavioral Problems   202

APPENDIXES
APPENDIX A: National Dog Associations
and Organizations   211

APPENDIX B: Magazines and Web Sites
of Interest   213

INTRODUCTION

Dogs and humans were made for each other. Long ago, we both entered into a mutually beneficial pact; in exchange for food, shelter, guidance, and companionship our canine friends agreed to serve us faithfully as hunters, herders, protectors, workers, and friends. To their credit, they have stuck by us through famine, drought, war, and all manner of hard times. Dogs have helped us become the successful creatures we are; for that we owe them our thanks.

Perhaps the most telling reward given to our canine partners just might be their de facto retirement from the very work they were bred to do. Now called upon to do few of the jobs they once performed, they have full membership in our own human pack. Once allowed into the home only for brief moments, our dogs now eat, sleep, and play away much of their lives under our roofs and in our company, as full-fledged members of our own families. While we continue to slave away, they stay put and take care of things until we come home. All we expect in return is love, companionship, and an occasional bark or two whenever uninvited salespersons come nosing around.

Unfortunately, this shift from worker to full-time housemate has not been an entirely effortless one for the dog, for a number of reasons. Human society as a whole tends to be far more democratically structured than that of the canine, whose rigidly hierarchical mind-set drives all dogs, good and bad, to strive for the highest pack position available. No dogs willingly reside at the bottom of their pack, unless it is made clear to them that there is where they belong. Many well-meaning, loving dog owners make the mistake of treating their canine friends as pack equals, with some going so far as to make their dogs the undeniable centers of attention. In doing so, they unknowingly allow their dogs to assume dominance over their human packs. When this occurs, all manner of behavioral problems can pop up, among them outright disobedience and even aggression toward the owner.

Other canine behavioral problems can also be blamed on the dog's changed status over the past few decades. With more and more families relying on two incomes to get by, domestic dogs now find themselves left at home alone, often for up to ten hours each day. No longer able to interact closely with their environment, these "latchkey" pets become isolated from others, a highly unnatural state for such a sociable animal. A plethora of behavior problems can result, including destructiveness, separation anxiety, house soiling, and many more.

Still more canine behavioral problems arise simply due to the failure of an owner to properly obedience train his or her dog. Left without rules or purpose, most dogs will make up their own or do whatever they feel like doing, often with disastrous results. These dogs never learn to truly think but instead simply react to stimuli, an undesirable situation for any owner, who will not be able to ever predict what his or her dog is going to do next.

Of the millions of dogs kept as domestic pets, a large percentage will develop behavioral problems sometime in their lives. A disobedient dog can create a great deal of stress and anger in the life of a dog owner, who, though endeared to the pet, cannot long tolerate the misbehavior.

Fortunately, the domestic dog is a very intelligent and adaptable creature. If Fido can learn to misbehave, *he can just as easily learn to behave.* Given the proper conditions, training, and motivation, almost all dogs can learn the error of their ways and begin to act in a more acceptable fashion. As easily as dogs can learn to sit or shake hand, they can learn to stop an unwanted behavior or allow it to be replaced by another.

That is what this book is all about. Providing the reader with easy-to-implement solutions to the most common and disruptive canine behaviors, *Bad Dog!* shows how to discourage unwanted canine behaviors and replace them with desirable ones. Part 1 is a valuable primer on basic canine needs, desires, and instincts. Part 2, the heart of the book, provides an A–Z listing of the most common and annoying canine behavioral problems a reader might experience with his or her dog. This comprehensive list defines each problem, explains why the dog is behaving badly, and offers easy-to-implement solutions that any owner can successfully apply to his or her misbehaving pooch. In addition, preventive measures are included, so that new dog owners can start their pets off right and prevent problems from ever arising.

None of the solutions offered in part 2 rely on *harsh, humiliating, or disrespectful methods;* instead, they focus on replacement behaviors, simple removal of undesirable stimuli, environmental adaptations, and benign leash techniques to achieve success. In this way, as little trauma as possible is created for both the owner and the dog. In fact, many of the reeducation techniques used are fun for all. This unique aspect (combined with the author's experience and past success) is what makes the techniques in *Bad Dog!* work so well.

Part 3, the final section, offers the reader ten succinct "commandments" that every owner should abide by when interacting with his or her dog to maintain a mutually beneficial relationship. When these commandments are combined with the problem-solving techniques in part 2 and the short primer on the canine mind in part 1, the reader gets a complete package, one that is sure to put his or her dog back onto the straight and narrow.

Filled with helpful hints and interesting insights into the

canine mind, *Bad Dog!* will give you the tools and the techniques to identify, understand, and eliminate most of your best friend's less desirable habits, freeing both of you to enjoy each other's company to the fullest, which is what dog ownership should be all about.

PART ONE

The Dog: What You Need to Know First

Dogs are among the world's smartest, most adaptable creatures. From the snow-white arctic fox or the remarkable wolf to the scavenging African hyena, canines range the planet, flourishing in nearly every climate and terrain. A clever survivor, masterful hunter, and devoted family member, the dog has a behavioral profile not unlike our own.

Perhaps because of the inherent similarities between human and canine psychology, we decided long ago to wrest dogs from their wild homes and put them to good use as hunters, trackers, herders, guardians, and companions. In exchange for their services we offered food, shelter, and companionship, perhaps the three most valued commodities in any animal's life. Eventually selective breeding techniques morphed the wild canine into the many domesticated breeds we are so familiar with today. Dogs specifically bred for hunting became fast and athletic, with high prey drives; those bred to track developed incredibly keen senses of smell. Whatever we humans had a need for, a dog breed was developed to fulfill it. The dog became a highly specialized tool, which, when put into the hands of the right trainer, could accomplish more than a host of humans ever could.

Over time, the number of domestic dog breeds increased dramatically, and now they number well over a hundred. That the Great Dane and the Chihuahua are the same species is testament to how effective the selective breeding process has been. Though size, appearance, temperament, and behavioral specialization may all vary tremendously, the basic drives and instincts of all domestic dog breeds remain relatively constant. A Saint Bernard and a border collie, though vastly different in personality and size, both share the same "pack" mentality, dictating that a leader, once identified, is obeyed and that the safety and well-being of the pack is the most important consideration.

When we took dogs out of the wild, it became necessary to train them. Herding dogs had to learn to look after their flocks and to obey the commands of the herders. The training was necessary not only to show the dogs what was expected but also to prevent them from killing the same animals they were herding. This was made possible by taking advantage of the dog's desire to please the leader of the pack, in this case the herder. The instinct to obey the leader was stronger than the desire to kill the sheep. By using dogs' innate respect for the dominance hierarchy we were able to train them to do virtually anything we desired. The jobs they were given to do became their purpose in life; instead of ranging the forests looking for game, the domestic dog did our bidding with the same desire and intensity.

Today, however, most domestic dogs are no longer called upon to do the jobs they were bred to do. Few collies now herd; fewer dalmatians run beside horse-drawn fire engines. Instead, the vast majority of domestic dogs are kept simply as companions and are considered valued members of their respective families. No longer required to work for a living, the breeds aren't asked to do much of anything except keep us company.

That's where the problems started. No longer asked to herd, guard, track, or retrieve, most dog breeds were left without a clear way to express their innate drives. Without ever seeing a herd of sheep, border collie puppies will still have the drive to herd. Without a way to express that desire, these dogs are apt to eventually act out in a way considered unacceptable by their owners.

In addition to having lost the jobs they were bred to perform, today's domestic dogs are also often treated by owners in a way that helps foster misbehavior. Many owners today do not understand how important the concept of a leader really is to a dog. No matter what the breed, dogs must feel a sense of leadership if they are to be expected to obey and behave. Without this, all dogs will instinctively strive to become the leaders of their "packs." When this happens, all manner of problem behaviors can occur. Dogs who think they are leaders act in a dominant fashion and feel they have the right to do whatever they want. This can include growling or snapping at members of the family (an example of a leader disciplining the pack), stealing food, pulling an owner down the street by the leash, not coming when called, or jealously coveting a bed or other piece of furniture. To dominant dogs these are all normal behaviors that are their right and responsibility to perform. By not providing your dog with leadership you create a situation whereby he must fill the position and play the role of boss himself.

Owners often force their dogs to fill the leadership role by treating the pets in the same manner they might treat human children. This democratic method might work with humans but not with dogs. Give your dog the same rights and privileges as yourself, and you tell her that she has equal status and therefore equal stature in the pack. Make her the center of attention, and you teach her that she is above you in the pack, a sure recipe for disaster. Spoiled and pampered dogs are especially likely to become dominant and pushy, because they assume they are receiving all of the attention due to their leadership status.

THE DOG'S BASIC DRIVES

In order to best understand what makes your dog tick, you must first comprehend what motivates him to do the things he does. What are his priorities? What basic drives are present, and how do they affect the animal's day-to-day behavior and his interactions with you? Developing a better understanding of your dog's instinctual needs and desires will open a window to the canine psyche for you, letting you see the reasons and motivations behind his actions, be they desirable or otherwise.

Food

Few drives remain as strong and important to the dog as the food, or predatory, drive. Eating is an essential, age-old drive for all animals, particularly the canine. Along with the drive to reproduce, the drive to find and consume food has been and continues to be the strongest motivator in the animal kingdom. From the ant to the human, to eat is to live.

Few predators have been as successful as the dog. Blessed with large brains, athletic bodies, and the superb ability to work together with other pack members, dogs have historically had few problems finding food. Obtaining food is a very serious and elemental drive, not only for the wild dog but for your pet as well. Domesticity has not dulled your canine friend's desire to eat. Recognize this, and you will be able to understand many aspects of your dog's everyday behavior, such as her desire to chase a squirrel or to instantly gobble up any food accidentally dropped onto the kitchen floor.

Though your dog has no real need to hunt for food, the instinct to do so is still relatively intact. If you have any doubts about this, simply observe the behavior of nearly any dog who comes upon a rabbit or squirrel in the woods. Even smaller breeds such as the Yorkshire terrier will become excited and motivated to catch the "prey." From the smallest dog to the largest, the desire to chase down and eat other animals remains.

Evidence of your dog's predatory drive can readily be seen around feeding time. Your dog will most likely savor her moments around the food dish and may greedily defend her access to it, showing varying signs of aggression when another pet comes too close to the bounty. This behavior can be especially common when a new dog is introduced into an established dog's domain and tries to weasel up to the food dish while the older dog is eating. This type of aggressive behavior, though unpleasant, is not necessarily abnormal and should not surprise an owner who attempts to introduce a new dog into the older one's home. Once the pecking order is firmly established, however, most dogs will allow another to be relatively close by during dinner, provided the new dog does not try to take the established dog's food from right under his or her nose.

Because eating is such a strong drive for your dog, you will be able to utilize it to help shape or change her behavior. You are the provider of that food, after all, and as such can use it to reinforce desirable behaviors and discourage undesirable ones. Most dogs if fed on a predictable schedule will respond quite well to food offerings and quickly learn whatever behavior is desired of them in exchange for a tasty tidbit.

Territory

In the wild, many canines are group hunters who stake out a hunting territory, then defend it from all other canine packs. The reason for doing so is clear and twofold. First, for predators such as dogs to survive, they must be assured of an adequate supply of prey. In order to achieve this, each pack must lay claim to a territory that holds a population of prey animals large enough to support the pack. Any smaller, and the dogs would not be able to survive and would instead have to invade the territory of another pack, a risky, life-threatening venture. A careful balance develops, then, between competing dog packs in the wild. Territorial boundaries are marked through the spraying of urine, defecation, and depositing scent from various glands on the animal's body. Through fear and respect these canine hunters maintain an uneasy understanding with neighboring competitors.

Though most canines in the wild tend to mate with members from within their own groups, some (such as the fox) live relatively isolated lives and must maintain a distinct territory to ensure that a high enough number of mates will be encountered. The larger the territory, the greater the opportunity to mate. Older or weaker males not able to maintain a large enough territory will not pass their genes along to future generations. Their lines will run out in favor of those of the stronger, more territorial canines.

Of the two, the maintenance of a sufficient supply of prey is the more important. The interesting factor in territorial drive is not the size of the territory, however, but the availability of prey. In situations where the density of prey animals is very high, territories can be quite small or even overlapping. For example, stray dogs living near a garbage dump might number in the dozens, due to the ready supply of food. These dogs become very tolerant of the presence of other dogs because of the abundance of food. Why fight and risk injury when there is enough for all? So, when food is plentiful dogs become less territorial and more tolerant of each other.

Though most domestic dogs have little or no need to hunt for their suppers, they nonetheless retain a fairly strong territorial drive. Understanding that this drive exists in all dogs will help you manage your own pet's behavior and respect her need for control over some territory. Recognizing your dog's territorial drive will help foster a safer, happier environment for her and for yourself. For example, being aware of your dog's territorial instincts will, I hope, deter you from impulsively bringing home a three-year-old male German shepherd, three abandoned cats, two guinea pigs, and a ferret.

Your dog will try to claim territory by barking, marking, or fighting with other animals who try to invade his space. Though these behaviors are predictable, they are not acceptable inside your home. How to deal with them is covered in detail later in the book. The territorial drive can be minimized somewhat, however, by raising your dog with as much socialization as possible and by making sure that food never becomes an issue of contention. A well-fed dog, after all, will be a much less contentious one.

Safety
All dogs want to live in a safe, secure environment. None of them enjoy abrupt changes in the normal flow of things. They want their everyday lives to be somewhat predictable and don't react well to constant perceived threats, such as sudden raps on the door, screaming children running through the home, thunder, or fireworks. To help prevent abnormal behaviors from surfacing in your dog, be aware of his basic need to feel comfortable and safe. Avoiding too many rowdy guests, deafening music, or constant changes in the home environment will go a long way in helping to keep your dog happy and problem-free.

Sex
The drive to mate and produce offspring is a strong one in all unneutered dogs. By the time a male or female is seven months old, he or she will begin to show a desire to do so. For those owners who do not have their dogs neutered, this drive can cause a number of unwanted behaviors. Males will want to roam; if allowed to do so, they could get into fights with other male dogs, possibly getting injured in the process. If limited to the home environment, the unneutered male will often mark in and around the house. Unneutered females allowed unsupervised access to the outdoors could ultimately become pregnant, repeatedly, and may also get into fights, particularly with other females. If kept indoors, the unneutered female could possibly mark or spot all over the house.

Fortunately, unwanted behavior due to the sex drive can be easily dealt with, simply by having your dog neutered by his or her sixth or seventh month. Castration for the male or spaying for the female will quickly quell most of these unwanted behaviors. Unless your dog has a prized pedigree, there really is no need to put off neutering. In addition to putting a halt to the aforementioned unwanted behaviors, neutering will actually help extend the life of your pet by preventing several types of cancer and by minimizing the chance of the dog getting into a life-threatening fight with another animal. In addition, having your dog neutered will help prevent one of the domestic canine's most pressing problems, namely, their rampant overpopulation. One visit to your local animal shelter will be all you'll need to convince yourself; there you will see dozens of unwanted puppies, produced by unneutered dogs procreating far in excess of what is necessary to maintain the species. When faced with a litter of unwanted puppies, many owners simply take the poor babies to the nearest shelter, thinking that they will be adopted quickly. Unfortunately, the supply far exceeds the demand, causing tens of thousands of puppies to be euthanized each year. Neutering your dog, perhaps more than any other act, will prevent many unwanted behavior problems and help put a halt to the ceaseless, unnecessary killing of innocent animals.

Parenting

The urge to care for the young is a strong drive in female dogs, as it is in all mammals. The desire to be loved and cared for is also strong, particularly among puppies, who crave the company and attention of their mother and littermates. Being aware of these drives will help you understand your dog better, in a number of ways. If your dog is a nursing mother, you will know to respect her space, especially when she is with her puppies. Keeping strangers and rambunctious children away from her while she is interacting with her litter will help prevent unnecessary stress or aggression and will allow the puppies to receive the motherly attentions they so dearly need, if they are to mature properly.

Dogs socialize with their own kind more during puppyhood than perhaps at any other time. This short eight-to-ten-week period of intense play and companionship with littermates is vital to puppies, because it teaches them all about canine manners and the structure of the pack and helps to minimize fear-aggressive tendencies later in life. Puppies taken from their mothers and littermates before the eighth week of life will often become antisocial adults, who cannot deal well with the company of other dogs and who will in all likelihood shun the attentions of most humans, save their owners.

Puppies also need to interact with their mothers and littermates for another important reason, namely, to develop a need for sibling and maternal attentions, which is usually transferred to the puppy's new human owner. Puppies who learn to love their mothers and respect their littermates will carry that love along with them to their new homes, making human contact a desirable thing in their life.

Play

Yes, playing is a normal drive in dogs, especially for puppies and adolescent dogs. Among puppies, it is a vital activity, as it helps develop their motor skills as well as their ability to interact properly with others of their own kind. Play is essential to a puppy's psychological and physiological development, as it is with all mammal babies.

During play, puppies learn all about the dominance hierarchy in the litter. A pecking order forms early on, and they need to discover where they fit in the scheme of things. Are they near the top of the litter or closer to the bottom? Being allowed to work this out through games of strength and possession is crucial to a dog's future sense of self and to developing tolerance of other dogs.

Through play, dogs learn to tolerate and enjoy physical touch. This helps teach dogs to tolerate being handled and groomed later in life, by their owners.

The drive to play also serves a crucial purpose for the mother, particularly among wild dogs. As she is forced to sometimes leave her babies to hunt for food, the litter with their playful antics serve as "baby-sitters" of sorts for one another, keeping them occupied while she is gone. In this way, the litter stays together until she comes back home with dinner. This behavior is especially true with canines such as the fox, which never travels in a pack and therefore has no fellow foxes available for "baby-sitting" duties.

Finally, the play instinct helps the puppies to learn about their immediate environment. During play, puppies will often explore their surroundings, a behavior that helps feed the animals' insatiable curiosity and teaches them valuable lessons about safety.

Curiosity

Most dogs have an instinctive need to explore or investigate, as do all intelligent creatures. Scrutinizing every little thing that comes into the line of sight is a natural reaction for any hunter. Through this instinct, dogs learn about their world and develop their intellect. Denied a stimulating environment, dogs can become antisocial, lethargic, and possibly destructive. You should always provide your dog with interesting, mentally stimulating things to see and do to ensure that he remains happy and healthy.

Rest

Dogs tend to spend nearly as much time sleeping or resting as they do being awake and active. An adult dog might spend as much as ten to twelve hours each day curled up in a sleepy ball on the carpet, dreaming of chasing cats or squirrels in the backyard. Though the reason for this is unclear, researchers believe that a puppy's brain develops most during sleep, necessitating the long periods of inactivity. This penchant for sleep is then carried over into adulthood. In addition, most dogs are quite active and alert while awake, perhaps requiring them to get more sleep than us.

◆　◆　◆

Acknowledging and understanding these basic canine drives will go a long way in helping you relate to your dog. You will be able to anticipate a larger number of his behaviors more easily and discern in advance just what his reaction to an upcoming situation will be. That is one of the goals of this book: if you can predict the inevitability of an undesirable behavior before it occurs, you can head it off at the pass, which is the best way to create a happy, problem-free relationship with your dog. If you know that dogs prefer stability in their environment, you might decide against adopting those three adorable basset hound puppies you saw at the shelter and bringing them home to your older dog. Or, being now aware of your dog's desire to protect his food, you might decide that allowing your two-year-old child to stick her face into your dog's dish while he eats is probably not a good idea. Being able to predict how your dog will react to any given situation is the first step in minimizing canine behavioral problems. Remember, prevention is preferable to behavior modification every time.

THE CANINE ANATOMY

Your dog is an incredible physical specimen. A direct descendant of the wolf and perhaps the jackal, the dog has the same basic anatomy, the same sensory abilities, and similar physical capabilities. Though centuries removed from the wild, many domestic dogs nevertheless look and act much like their ancient ancestors, with some (like the German shepherd and the malamute) seemingly little changed.

Dogs' marvelous anatomy allow them to perform amazing physical feats. They are swift and tireless runners. They can leap high and wide and maneuver with great agility, turning on a dime whenever necessary. They can hear a pin drop and can smell an open can of dog food from half a mile away. Truly well-designed predators.

The domestic dog can vary in size tremendously, due to selective breeding techniques used by us over the centuries. A teacup Chihuahua can weigh less than five pounds, while a Saint Bernard can tip the scales at over two hundred pounds. The average dog usually weighs in at around forty to fifty pounds and measures eighteen to twenty-two inches at the withers (or shoulders). Dogs have forty-two teeth (as opposed to the cat's thirty), including molars to crush bone with and sharp canines to puncture and tear flesh. The dog's hair can vary from the short single coat of the boxer, to the dense double coat of the malamute, to the long, straight, luxurious locks of the Afghan. The coat of the dog helps regulate body temperature but also serves as a first line of defense from bites, as well as potentially harmful plant thorns or brambles. In addition, it helps prevent dehydration and keeps harmful ultraviolet rays off the animal's skin.

Domestic dogs have five keen senses, which allow them to interact with their world. Of the five, the canine sense of smell is definitely the most acute. A dog can detect odors that we are completely unaware of, from distances of up to a mile or more. This ability has long been harnessed and used by us in the tracking and hunting professions, as well as in rescue and drug or bomb detection. Dogs' eyesight, designed to detect movement better than ours, does not discern details as well as the human eye and does not detect colors nearly as well (though dogs are not totally color-blind). The reason for this is simply that canines do not need to see colors to survive, whereas humans do, to locate colorful fruits and vegetables and to distinguish brightly colored poisonous foods and animals from less dangerous ones. Dogs are mostly carnivorous and need eyesight that specializes in catching dull-colored, fast-moving prey. Canines, much like felines, have the ability to see much better in the dark than we do, due to the *tapetum lucidum*, a reflective coating behind the retina, which reflects back onto the retina any light not absorbed the first time around. This allows dogs to use more of the available light and allows them to see under lighting conditions that we would consider pitch-black. The *tapetum lucidum* also gives the dog's eyes that captivating "glow in the dark" feature, also present in other species, including the cat, whose ability to see in the dark exceeds even that of the dog.

Dogs have excellent hearing, a product of having to listen for the nearly silent movements of prey animals roaming about. Capable of hearing sounds much higher in frequency than we can, the dog often detects an approaching person or animal well before we do.

The dog's sense of taste is also well developed, though no taste buds for sweetness exist on the canine tongue. Carnivores like the dog have little need to detect sweetness, unlike vegetarians and omnivores, who routinely eat plant materials that have moderate to high levels of sugar in them.

The canine sense of touch, though not as well developed as our own, is important nonetheless. Dogs have touch receptors on their skin and especially on their foot pads and nose, allowing them to probe an object and sense whether it is hot or cold, soft or hard, rough or smooth.

Though dogs cannot move quite as fast as cats, they have much more endurance and can run seemingly forever, as evidenced by the wild dogs of Africa, who are able to track and follow much faster prey for hours if need be, until the animal is exhausted. This ability to perform physically over a long span of time allows the dog to be a much stronger swimmer than the cat, who, though faster in the short run, does not have the stamina of the dog.

THE DOG/OWNER RELATIONSHIP: WHO ARE WE TO THEM?

As mentioned before, the reasons for owning a dog have changed significantly over the last hundred years. No longer needed to help on the farm or in the fields, most dogs are now kept solely as companions. So, just what do these companion dogs think of us?

Ideally, they think of us as leaders and as parental figures. Dogs are programmed to seek out that type of guidance; in fact, they savor it. When provided with proper leadership, dogs are much more apt to behave in a respectful manner toward us and toward the "territories" they live in.

Unfortunately, many dog owners give away this leader/parent status or else never establish it at all. When this happens, an owner becomes a subordinate littermate in the eyes of his or her dog. Without an effective leader/parent present, dogs sense the "vacuum" of power and will in most cases attempt to fill the position themselves, resulting in all sorts of behavioral problems. The relationship changes from a respectful, controlled one to one that often results in the owner becoming controlled, bullied, or ignored by the dog, who honestly thinks that he or she is now in charge.

When an owner is ignorant of his or her dog's instincts and needs, behavior problems become a certainty. The kindhearted but misguided owner who insists on establishing a democratic relationship with his or her pet shows a basic lack of understanding of canine psychology and courts disaster. Any dog in the world, if given a chance to control his or her environment, will do so, to the disadvantage of the hapless owner.

When an owner sets clear rules and boundaries, enforces those rules, and treats the dog in a fair, predictable fashion, odds are his or her leadership will not be questioned. But when dogs are allowed to set the rules and to behave in whatever manner they choose, the owners become the owned and the dogs are left with the daunting responsibility of running things. That is a difficult task for animals with the reasoning power of a two-year-old human child.

THE IMPORTANCE OF UNDERSTANDING A DOG'S NEEDS AND DESIRES

In order to be happy, healthy, and free of undesirable behaviors, your dog needs to have certain basic needs met. Most owners are aware of some, while other needs might not be so obvious. As one of the main themes of this book is prevention, it makes sense to briefly talk about what a dog's basic needs and desires might be. Doing your best to provide your dog with all of them can help prevent a host of problems before they ever surface.

Food

An obvious one, as your dog needs to have sufficient food each day in order to stay happy and healthy not only for nutritional reasons but also to satisfy his food/prey drive. Most owners supply their dogs with more than enough food. As much care must be taken, however, with regard to the quality of the food as to the quantity. A dog who eats plenty of poor-quality food will become just as malnourished as a dog who doesn't eat enough quality food. Without the right nutrition, a dog will suffer and show both physiological and behavioral signs of it.

Shelter

Another no-brainer, as all dogs need to be sheltered from inclimate weather, harsh temperatures, or any other severe conditions that might threaten their health and well-being. Dogs forced to brave the elements or forced to exist under dangerous or unhealthy conditions could become sick or injured. As an owner, your job is to see that this does not occur.

Stability

Though it is impractical to expect you to never change your environment, keep in mind that, in doing so, you should expect your dog to react to the change in some way. Ideally, keep the status quo as long as possible, to avoid unexpected surprises. This includes not only the physical environment of your pet, but the structure of her day as well. For example, if you are never home during the day, then suddenly change to working nights, your dog may react to it in some way, be it a temporary change of mood, a quick bout of house-training mishaps, or something equally undesirable.

This goes for bringing in new pets as well. Though dogs generally are far more accepting of new pets than are cats, your dog needs to feel as loved and wanted as possible, particularly when a new pet is introduced. If your dog is very territorial, she may react aggressively toward the newcomer. House-training mishaps and destruction to your property are also possible. Even bringing a new person into the home can subtly alter your dog's behavior for a while, until she becomes used to the new person, which can be difficult for some dogs, especially the shy, timid types.

The bottom line is, change what must be changed but otherwise keep the status quo. This will allow your dog to feel the stability she instinctively seeks in her environment. If change is inevitable, try to introduce it as slowly as possible, to make it more acceptable to your dog.

Leadership

Your dog must feel that you are a capable, caring, and fair leader. Without this, she will feel insecure and will probably be forced to take over the reins of power. Don't let it happen; be a good leader, in order to create a happy, secure mind-set in your pooch.

THE IMPORTANCE OF OBEDIENCE TRAINING

Training your dog to obey a number of simple commands is a necessary part of dog ownership. In addition to helping you establish leadership, the ability to control your dog's movements and actions could one day save her life. No worse feeling in the world exists than having your disobedient dog wander out into a busy street or run away while on a camping trip far from home. Teaching her to obey a few key obedience commands such as *sit, down, stay, heel,* and *come* will also make your life much easier, by giving you control and authority over your dog.

Consider signing up for an obedience class in your area as soon as possible, especially if you and your dog are having a problem with leadership and dominance issues. The Humane Society and the SPCA (Society for the Prevention of Cruelty to Animals) both offer classes, as do many local animal shelters. Privately run canine obedience schools in your area also hold classes on a regular basis. Look in the yellow pages to find one near you.

In obedience class, your dog should learn the aforementioned commands, plus how to walk on a loose leash and how to properly greet people (without jumping on them). Most classes also discuss canine behavior theories, nutrition, games, and leadership. Another big plus to taking a class is the socialization your pooch will get while there, with both dogs and people. Most classes have over a dozen dogs and owners milling about; most dogs never get to be around this type of crowd and instead see only a few persons each day. Socialization is a key ingredient in building your dog's confidence and in teaching her how to pay attention to you even though many distractions are present.

Once your dog graduates from obedience class, you need to keep up on her newfound training by working all of the commands regularly in different locations. Don't just have her perform the commands at home; work on them in a park, on the street, or even in a friend's backyard. You must be able to get her to obey you under all circumstances and not just in the familiar, quiet surroundings of your home.

After the obedience class, consider taking a tricks and agility class, usually available at the same institution. Many dogs love the positive, fun atmosphere and enjoy performing all of the interesting tasks at hand, such as jumping over hurdles, running through tunnels, weaving in between poles, and performing tricks such as fetch, catch, roll over, speak, and many others.

Once your dog's obedience training is solidly established, consider entering her into an obedience competition. Sponsored by either organizations such as the AKC (American Kennel Club) or the UKC (United Kennel Club) or numerous local mixed-breed dog clubs, the competitions are normally organized in a three-tiered fashion: *novice* level, the intermediate *open* level, and the more advanced *utility* level. Those dogs that pass the novice class are awarded a CD, or "companion dog," certificate (or a UCD, in an event sponsored by the UKC). Those passing the open class are awarded the CDX, or "companion dog excellent," certificate (called the UCDX by the UKC). Those highly trained dogs who pass the utility class requirements are awarded the UD, or "utility dog," certificate (called the UUD by the UKC). As a plus, any dog smart enough to pass one or more of these stringent obedience tests is highly unlikely to have any significant behavior problems at home.

Whatever level of training your dog completes, the important thing to know is that she needs training to feel a sense of purpose and to learn that you are the leader of your "pack." Once your dog sees you in that light, she will want to obey and please you. That is the secret to preventing and eliminating canine behavioral problems. Remember that it is better to lead a willing dog than it is to force your will upon a dominant pet.

THINKING LIKE A DOG: UNDERSTANDING WHY BAD BEHAVIORS OCCUR

Whenever some behavior of your dog clashes with your expectations, he is said to be misbehaving. The dog might not think of his behavior as being improper, though; in fact, he might not see anything wrong with it at all. For instance, marking and chasing behaviors are all natural, normal behaviors for dogs, both wild and domestic. For your dog to hungrily chase your cat around the house seems absolutely par for the course to him. He in no way means to be malicious. It is simply an expression of his normal instincts.

Domestication of any animal tends to go against Mother Nature's natural programming. When you ask your dog not to perform an instinctive behavior, you are going up against millions of years of evolution. So, one major cause of misbehavior in a dog is not the pet's desire to consciously annoy you but your inability to find a way for your dog to express those natural instincts in an acceptable way or to cleverly let the animal know what the new rules are concerning good and bad behavior in the home.

A good way to help minimize bad behaviors in your dog is to try to think like she does. If you were a dog, wouldn't you find that tiny hamster a tremendous temptation, especially with it sitting atop the easily accessible desk or dresser, in a small glass enclosure? Sure you would. Why wouldn't you? Scratch one hamster. This terrible "misbehavior" could have been easily avoided by you looking around the home through the eyes of your dog and seeing all the temptations. The hamster should have been located in a dog-proof area, well out of reach. End of problem before it starts.

Remember that your dog has the reasoning capacity of a two-year-old child. You wouldn't expect a toddler to behave like an adult, would you? Your dog will never go beyond that intellectual stage, so do not assume he can discern an adult human's conception of right and wrong. Instead, set up your dog's environment so that as little trouble as possible can be gotten into by him.

In addition to prevention, other ways to avoid misbehaviors in dogs exist. Again, think like a dog; do you want to have absolutely nothing to do all day? All dogs need some form of mental stimulation to keep themselves occupied and out of trouble. If you do not supply your dog with adequate and acceptable distractions, she will find ways to entertain herself that might not meet with your approval. The bored dog will end up getting into cupboards, closets, and other areas you consider off-limits, simply out of a need to satisfy her instinct to be curious about her environment. Get down on all fours and think like a dog; what is there to investigate?

A good rule of thumb with any dog is: if it's there, the dog will find it. So, thinking like your dog again, look around the home and see if you can spot items that she might want to investigate. *Well, look at that, a turkey leg left on the counter. Guess I'll just jump on up there and eat some of it.* Then you come out of the bathroom, find the food half-eaten and on the floor, and proceed to yell at the dog. Bad move. The whole thing was your fault. You should punish yourself! Next time, put the food where your pooch can't get to it. Remove it from her environment, and the undesirable behavior won't occur.

Use this logic as often as possible. Dog-proof the home. Remove anything you value from your dog's environment. Food? In your mouth or in the refrigerator. Houseplants? Hang them, put them in metal stands, or move them to a safe room. Anything that your dog has had a history of getting into remove from her domain. It's often as simple as that.

If you first make an effort to understand the root causes of your dog's misbehavior, then take steps to prevent it from occurring again, you and your canine friend will have a much happier relationship. Just remember that the dog isn't acting out of malice or spite; she's just doing what she thinks is necessary and what her instincts tell her to do. Thinking like a dog and staying one step ahead of her will cut most bad behaviors off at the pass.

THE EFFECTS OF BREED ON BEHAVIOR

As stated earlier, amazingly, the Chihuahua and the Saint Bernard are the same species. They certainly do not act alike, however. Except for sharing the basic canine drives, each dog breed has a unique temperament that sets it apart from all the others. Golden retrievers, for instance, are an extremely sociable, active breed, whereas a saluki is an aloof, reserved dog preferring not to interact with those outside the immediate family.

Many owners can run into problems when the breed-specific behavior of their dogs begins to clash with their lifestyles, personalities, and expectations. Herding dogs such as border collies, for instance, might not be the best breeds for a family with small children, as the dog may try to herd them as if they were sheep, nipping at their heels in the process or chasing them down the street. Though training can modify the behavior, the instincts will always be there, tugging at the dog. That family would do better with a retriever, as they love children and will endure almost limitless amounts of attention from them without becoming worried or annoyed.

Those who purchase a dog for purely aesthetic reasons may end up with a pet whose behavior conflicts with their lifestyle. Problems such as chasing cars, biting, barking, or dominance can result from making the wrong choice. Incredibly, the AKC currently recognizes 147 different dog breeds. In addition, many other breeds exist worldwide that have not yet been officially recognized by the AKC. This amazing variation can often make choosing a purebred dog a confusing quest.

The breeds are divided into seven distinct groups, plus a Miscellaneous group, which includes breeds waiting for AKC approval. Each group contains dog breeds sharing common behavioral profiles; knowing these may aid you in choosing properly. The following sections list the seven existing groups and give a general behavioral profile for each. Individual dog breeds within each group can be researched by you at the bookstore or library or on-line. Consider purchasing a book dedicated to choosing a dog breed or contacting the AKC for more information.

The Sporting Group

Dogs in this group include pointers, setters, spaniels, and retrievers. Bred to assist hunters in finding, flushing, and retrieving game, these breeds have great stamina and high activity levels. Few would do well in an apartment setting. Owners of a dog in the sporting group will need to exercise their pets every day and ideally give them a job to do that resembles what they were bred for. Fetching and swimming are two great pastimes for these pooches. Dogs in this group usually do well with children but need an active owner who enjoys a busy dog.

The Hound Group

This group includes both scent hounds and sight hounds. Scent hounds such as the bloodhound and basset hound were bred to track prey using their incredible noses. Scent hounds are high-energy dogs who can become easily distracted by any unusual scents wafting by. Though normally sweet, they can be hard to train due to their fixation on smells. Scent hounds require an owner to be firm yet understanding. Sight hounds, among the oldest of breeds, track prey not with their noses but with their keen eyesight. Greyhounds, salukis, borzois, and whippets are all members of this group. These dogs are fast as lightning and often aloof with strangers. Sight hounds require a patient owner.

The Working Group

An ancient group, these breeds were bred to help us perform difficult, strenuous tasks, such as sled pulling, rescue work, herd guarding, and homestead protection. They are smart, strong, dominant dogs with great courage and stamina and can often exhibit a high level of territoriality. These dogs require a strong-minded owner with great leadership skills. Breeds in this group include the mastiff, the rottweiler, the malamute, the Great Pyrenees, the akita, the Newfoundland, and the Saint Bernard.

The Terrier Group

Breeds in this group are sturdy and driven, with a high prey drive. Originally bred to kill vermin, they are intelligent, stubborn dogs that make great pets, provided the owner remains firm, fair, and determined. Breeds in this group include the schnauzer, the Airedale, the cairn terrier, the Scottish terrier, and the fox terrier.

The Toy Group

Dogs in this group were bred solely as companion or lap dogs. Small in stature, they tend to live a long time. As toy dogs are often strong-willed, the owner must be firm and should socialize them from an early age to combat their antisocial tendencies toward persons outside the family. Breeds in this group include the Chihuahua, the Maltese, the miniature pinscher, the Pekingese, and the Pomeranian.

The Nonsporting Group

As this group consists of dissimilar breeds that no longer have any clearly defined purpose other than companionship, most of these breeds cannot easily fit into any of the other groups. Most are a challenge to train and may not be extremely sociable, with a few exceptions. The owner of one of these breeds needs to socialize and train their dogs early and should never give unearned praise. Dogs in this group include the Chinese shar-pei, the chowchow, the Dalmatian, the Lhasa Apso, and the bulldog.

The Herding Group

Perhaps the most intelligent of the breed groups, these dogs have served for thousands of years as herders of sheep and cattle. These are normally great pets, but with an intelligence that often allows them to outthink their owners. Owners of a herding breed must give these active dogs some type of outlet for their energies and should obedience-train early. Breeds in this group include the Australian shepherd, the German shepherd, the collie, and the Shetland sheepdog.

A WORD ON MIXED-BREED DOGS

Mixed-breeds, or "mutts," are normally no better or worse than purebred dogs with regard to temperament and physiology. Remember that a mixed-breed dog is simply the product of purebred animals. Some persons insist that mixed-breed dogs are hardier than purebreds because they come from a larger gene pool, but this is not generally true (unless severe inbreeding was used to produce a purebred litter). If today's mixed-breed dogs were further removed from their purebred ancestors—say six or seven generations—there might be some validity to the claim. But this is not the case; the majority of "mutts" alive today have at least one purebred parent or grandparent, causing them to be very close in temperament and physiology to purebreds.

That said, mixed-breed dogs make great pets and are always available for little or no money, often at the nearest shelter. The only drawback to selecting mixed-breed dogs is not knowing much (or anything) about their bloodlines. When you buy a purebred, you often get to see the dog's parents and littermates, a great aid in determining the pup's adult temperament. Most mixed-breed dogs are available at an older age and rarely are their parents or littermates around for you to peruse.

Normally you can make a good guess at what purebred dogs went into creating a mutt. You can never be sure, though, making temperament predictions difficult. Nevertheless, mixed-breeds usually make wonderful, loyal pets. Before spending hundreds on a purebred, consider saving a mutt's life.

TECHNIQUES FOR ENDING BAD BEHAVIORS

One good way to change your dog's behavior is to convince him that it is *his choice to change*. Let him think it is all his decision. For instance, if your bored, homebound dog has gotten into the habit of climbing up onto the sofa to nap, you can try to redirect his behavior by introducing a comfortable plastic dog crate into the home. Placed in a warm, quiet location, a crate can often act as a security blanket for a dog. Placing a soft blanket inside, as well as a piece of your own clothing (such as an old T-shirt or sock), will give your dog a place to go that feels secure and homey. Placing a few treats inside the crate will also encourage him to go in for the first time. By taking advantage of the dog's denning instinct, you give him an alternative to getting his hair all over the sofa. The key to this solution is that the dog thinks that *he made the choice to leave the sofa alone,* in favor of the comfy, secure crate. Because he decided to redirect himself, there is no confrontational stress or trauma involved. End of problem; everyone is happy. You *prevented* the offensive behavior by *distracting* your dog's attention from the sofa and helping redirect it to the crate.

Another effective tactic is to identify the cause of an offensive behavior and *remove* it from the pet's environment. If your dog has taken to digging up one of your houseplants, all you need do is remove it from the pet's environment or else make all plants inaccessible to him. Then, if you like, you can redirect your dog's behavior by supplying him with a place outside where digging is allowed. Again, there was no confrontation between you and the dog; as far as he knows, it was all his decision.

Another way to change your dog's behavior nonconfrontationally is to *desensitize* her to a potentially upsetting stimulus. If she seems to be rather shy around another person, you might try having that person come over on a regular basis at dinnertime and prepare to serve the dog her food. She will quickly begin to associate the presence of that new person with what might be her favorite time of the day and eventually grow to look forward to the "interloper's" presence. The reserved behavior is modified in a nonconfrontational way.

When passive, nonconfrontational methods fail, mild forms of *discouragement* may need to be utilized to end the offensive behavior. For instance, if, despite the fact that you have supplied your dog with numerous chew toys throughout the home, she insists on continuing to chew on your favorite slippers, a timely squirt of water from a spray bottle or water pistol can help minimize or end the behavior. The beauty of the spray bottle technique is that the unpleasant consequence (namely, the stream of water) in no way jeopardizes the trust the dog has in you. Dogs who are physically abused by their owners become fearful of them and will never feel at ease again when their masters are close by. This sabotages the dog/owner relationship. The squirt of water, though shocking, is a separate entity from your own body. Even combining it with a firm *No!* command won't cause your dog to fear your presence or touch. He will only become conditioned to the word itself, quickly realizing that *No!* means *"You are doing something wrong and should stop it now."* The dog will quickly end the undesirable behavior to avoid the mysterious stream of water.

To review, minimizing undesirable behaviors in your dog (while still maintaining a good relationship with her) requires some thinking ahead, and a real understanding of the canine psyche. To effectively modify a dog's behavior, you should try these techniques, in the following order:

1. *Prevent,* by not introducing disturbing stimuli into the dog's environment.
2. *Distract,* by introducing a better, more acceptable stimulus.
3. *Remove,* if possible, whatever stimulus is causing the inappropriate behavior.
4. *Desensitize* your dog to whatever is causing her to misbehave.
5. *Discourage* her from behaving improperly, by using benign, impersonal methods such as water pistol squirts from across the room.

WHY OVERT PUNISHMENT DOESN'T WORK WELL

To live happily with your dog, you must develop a bond of mutual trust. He must know that *at no time* will you physically abuse or frighten him. Mistreat your dog once, and he may fear you for a long time. He may not necessarily stop the offending behavior, either, and could develop a few more as a result of the confrontation. Some dogs tend to "shut down" when presented with any type of ultimatum or overt threat. If you scream at your dog or swat him off the sofa with your hand, he may turn off his cognitive processes and begin to fear you. Instead of ending the undesirable behavior, you will harm the relationship and create stress in his life. The *only* time you should ever consider yelling at or striking your dog is if the pet is in the process of physically harming you or a loved one or about to do something perilous to his own health. Otherwise, remain calm, and treat your dog as if he were a two-year-old child.

THE EFFECTS OF HEALTH ON BEHAVIOR

Unlike humans, dogs tend to be rather stoic when it comes to showing pain or discomfort. They hide sickness and injury well; often an owner won't have a clue that his or her dog is ill or hurting in any way. Even a dog struck by a car will often show no obvious signs of injury, save an increased desire to sleep or a sudden need to hide away somewhere.

Many unusual and undesirable canine behaviors can be caused by some form of physical problem. The stress your dog feels from being sick or injured can often drive her to act in an unusual way. For instance, many dogs, upon contracting some type of viral or bacterial infection, may suddenly begin to have house-training problems. Other than this symptom, however, the dog might not show any outward signs of illness.

Before trying to correct some undesirable behavior in your dog, consider the fact that she may be suffering from illness or injury. Many unusual behaviors can be halted and corrected simply by having your veterinarian perform an examination. Doing so could end the undesirable behavior and possibly save your dog's life. Always ensure that your pooch is healthy before trying to effect some behavioral change.

To do so, you need to have a competent, caring veterinarian available. What qualities should you look for in a veterinarian? Beyond having a true love for animals, he or she should:

◆ Be knowledgeable and have a desire to keep up with the latest trends in pet health care.

◆ Communicate well with owners and never seem rushed, impatient, or rude.

◆ Allow you to be present during your dog's preliminary examination (though do not expect to be able to stick around during surgeries or any type of emergency procedure).

◆ Be organized and professional. The premises should not be dirty or chaotic, and the staff should be polite and helpful.

◆ Set reasonable fees. Though cost is often the furthest thing from your mind when your pet is ill, it nevertheless can become an issue. Veterinarians who charge outrageous fees for standard procedures such as neutering or vaccinating should be avoided, as should budget, high-volume clinics that appear too inexpensive to be true.

Finding a good veterinarian can often be as easy as getting a referral from a trusted friend or relative. Talking to your local shelter or listening to your breeder's advice can also be a good way to locate a competent veterinarian. You can even look in the local yellow pages, though this can often be a hit-and-miss affair and will require you to visit several clinics in advance in order to make an enlightened choice.

Once you have found an acceptable veterinarian, be sure to take your dog in for an annual checkup, to head off illness at the pass and to ensure the continuation of your pet's good health. Take your dog in once a year, even if he appears in perfect health. The doctor will check all of his vital signs, examine him for any abnormal lumps, growths, or parasites, and listen to him heart and lungs. The veterinarian might also perform blood, fecal, or urine tests to confirm good health or to catch a problem before it becomes serious. Vaccinations will also be given to ensure that your pet is immunized against all possible life-threatening contagions. This is especially important for dogs spending lots of time outdoors.

HAVING FUN INTERACTING WITH YOUR DOG

Clearly, the best way to ensure that your dog will not develop any irritating behaviors is to prevent them from ever starting. Keying in on your pet's needs, health, and instincts and taking steps to remove any and all undesirable items or situations from the dog's environment will go a long way toward guaranteeing a trouble-free relationship between you both. In addition, teaching your dog what is acceptable or unwanted behavior, while at the same time maintaining a trusting, mutually beneficial relationship, will be the other important factor in helping to reduce or eliminate undesirable canine behaviors.

If your dog exhibits one or more of the behavior problems listed in part 2 of this book, it won't be the end of the world. Each listing will clearly lay out for the reader the steps he or she will need to take to eliminate the problem, as well as a way to prevent it from ever reoccurring. Throughout the process of ridding your dog of one or more of these behavioral problems, try not to become too serious or confrontational; remember that she is just a dog, with limited reasoning capacity. She doesn't initially know that the behavior is improper. Look upon the situation as an opportunity to learn about your dog and yourself. See it as a valuable learning experience that opens up a window on canine instincts and behavior that might have previously been closed to you. Try to enjoy the experience; no one says you can't have fun reeducating your dog. The key to success is keeping things in perspective and making sure that both you and your pet have a good time learning about each other. In doing so, you will develop an even closer bond with your pooch.

PART TWO

Dog Behavior Problems, A–Z

This section is the heart of the book. It lists the most common behavior problems evident in today's domestic dogs and offers solutions that any owner should be able to implement. Each alphabetical listing will include:

1. The *name* of the undesirable behavior.
2. A detailed *description* of the behavior, enabling the dog owner to quickly determine if this is what his or her pet is doing wrong.
3. An explanation of why the problem is occurring, to aid you in understanding the behavior from the dog's perspective.
4. An easily implemented *solution* designed to minimize the offending behavior and prevent it from reoccurring. *Preventive* suggestions that will block the behavior from surfacing will also be mentioned here.

AGGRESSION

DESCRIPTION

Aggression can be defined as an offensive or defensive attack on an animal or human, with the intention of dominating, scaring off, intimidating, hurting, or even killing the unfortunate "invader." Several different types of aggression might be seen in a domestic dog, including:

1. *Dominance/territorial aggression,* in which the offending dog uses force or intimidation to control others and to possess whatever he or she desires.
2. *Fear aggression,* in which the dog attacks when frightened.
3. *Food aggression,* in which the dog attacks in order to protect his or her food or to take that of another.
4. *Hereditary aggression,* caused by faulty breeding.
5. *Maternal aggression,* in which a canine mother defends her puppies.
6. *Prey aggression,* as evidenced by a dog chasing and/or killing another animal.
7. *Play aggression,* usually evidenced by a puppy or adolescent dog.
8. *Redirected aggression,* in which a stressed dog lashes out at an innocent.

Make no mistake about it; dogs that growl, nip, bite, or seriously injure other animals or humans present their owners with a serious problem. When this kind of behavior occurs, most owners would do well to immediately consult a professional canine behaviorist rather than try to go it alone, which can (and often will) result in serious injury, as well as a heightening of the behavior.

Owners who live with an aggressive pet live lives of quiet desperation, planning their days and nights around the offending animal and limiting their own contact with the outside world in order to prevent disasters from occurring. Rather than enjoying the companionship a dog can give, these terrorized owners cloister themselves and their dogs in hopes of avoiding the inevitable aggressive episode. By doing so, these victims make the problem worse, due in part to the dog sensing his or her control over the owner's lifestyle and to the total lack of socialization in the dog's life, a great accelerator of aggressive behavior.

Sometimes aggression isn't a symptom of a disturbed pet but instead an understandable and proper response to certain situations. For instance, if your dog is nursing puppies and a happy-but-foolish golden retriever comes bounding into the room to investigate, that silly young canine is going to feel that mother dog's wrath mighty quickly, and rightly so. She is totally within her rights to protect her puppies from what she deems a possible threat to them. In this case, the maternal aggression shown by her would be totally justifiable and natural.

Though some aggression is explainable and normal, other forms of aggression can be quite abnormal. Timid dogs might, for instance, fear anything out of the ordinary and react aggressively when they needn't. For example, timid dogs have been known to bite human babies or toddlers, who, though meaning no overt harm, can seem very unpredictable and threatening to an inherently fearful dog.

Overly dominant dogs might actually go out of their way to attack another animal (or even a human) if they feel that their status or territory is being threatened in some way. Allowable in the wild, perhaps, this behavior is not welcome within the confines of domesticity. Domestication, in fact, is the key factor that can bring dog aggression to the forefront; with our desire to tame and subjugate our dogs to life in a home filled with adults, children, visitors, other pets, noise, and all manner of "unnatural" stimuli (from the dog's point of view) we have unintentionally created a potentially stressful environment for them, as the human home does not contain the same behavioral caveats found in the wild.

Whether normal or abnormal, canine aggression can be very upsetting to an owner who does not understand it or is not prepared for it. How an owner reacts to his or her dog's aggression is also an important issue; overreaction or improper responses can actually intensify the aggression problem.

WHY YOUR DOG IS DOING THIS

Dominance/territorial aggression occurs whenever dogs feel their status or territory is being usurped by another animal, usually a dog (but sometimes a human). The aggressor will show an initial suspicion of the intruder, regardless of how friendly he or she appears to be. The aggressive dog will growl at, chase, or physically attack the intruder.

Dominance and territorial aggression toward an owner might be exhibited in a number of ways, in and around the home. If your dog thinks himself the leader of his pack, he will claim areas or objects as his own and jealously guard them. He may growl or bite when asked to remove himself from your bed or chair or when you attempt to handle his food bowl. He might steal and covet an object of clothing and bite whoever tries to retrieve it. In extreme cases, he might even show some form of aggression when a family member tries to leave the room against the dog's wishes or if he is awakened suddenly. Dominant, aggressive dogs may decide to bite when an owner attempts to groom them, or examine their bodies.

Children roughhousing with dominant dogs are often nipped or bitten, because the dogs may suddenly interpret the physical jousting as a challenge to their perceived dominance. Even being touched or petted in a certain place can illicit a growl, nip, or bite from some dogs, who may feel that the area touched was "off-limits". Dominant dogs will often show aggression when a person attempts to handle their feet or look in their ears or mouths.

Territorial aggression can also be exhibited by dogs left in cars while their owners are in a store shopping. Such dogs may bark and growl at anyone coming too close to the car. Some dogs will even become territorial while being walked by their owners, in effect saying to other dogs or persons: *Stay out of my face, you! This is our small space, and I don't want you in it!*

Your home is your pooch's territory; any time an unknown creature comes around, it will initially be seen by your dog as an intruder. Though most domesticated dogs won't necessarily apply this rationale to human visitors, they may and might even bark a bit upon seeing the stranger's approach.

Though each dog will show a differing level of reaction to an "invader," odds are most won't be too thrilled at suddenly having to share territory with another animal. Some level of territorial posturing, at least in the beginning, should be expected. Though it may not escalate past growling or nipping, it could, and you need to be prepared for that.

Apart from territorial concerns, your dog will want to express his status, or dominance, over an intruding animal (or person). Dogs are very motivated by hierarchical concerns when placed into any social situation. Whenever two or more adult dogs get together, for instance, they will immediately begin working out who is the more dominant. Your dog will play this dominance posturing game with other dogs as well as with humans (though the humans often don't know it's happening until it's too late).

Dog aggression caused by dominance or territorial issues is a serious matter, particularly when directed at humans. Though possible solutions to the problem follow, it is highly recommended that you see a professional canine behaviorist as soon as possible, particularly if the behavior has existed for a prolonged period of time.

Fear aggression can be caused by a number of factors. Your dog retains all of the "fight or flight" instincts present in his wilder brethren; if he becomes frightened of something, he will either run away and hide or else confront the perceived threat in an effort to preserve his safety. What your dog decides is threatening, however, is a relative thing; a reserved, cautious Italian greyhound might become unnerved by the same thing that a more outgoing Labrador retriever finds a load of fun. It is all up to the dog.

Fear-aggressive dogs may attempt to bite anyone or anything that comes inside what they decide is their "safe space." Should a person, child, dog, or other pet try to approach too closely, the fear-aggressive dog may snarl, growl, or bite the perceived intruder.

Fear aggression can also stem from a genetic predisposition for it. If, for instance, one or both parents of a puppy have exhibited regular signs of fear aggression, odds are the puppy will, too.

The level of socialization that puppies receive while still in their litters plays a huge role in determining whether or not they will show signs of excess fear aggression later in life. Puppies separated from the litter before the eighth week, for instance, often become antisocial, fearful, and timid adults. The fifth through the eighth weeks are especially crucial; during this time, they learn how to properly interact with other dogs. If robbed of this key experience, a dog will almost always suffer from some form of behavioral problem later on.

Bad experiences can also trigger fear aggression in a dog. Dogs have long memories; if a young child accidentally trips over your ten-week-old puppy, injuring him in the process, the pet will remember the experience and very likely be uneasy around children in the future. Likewise, an otherwise well adjusted dog attacked by another dog will most likely show profound fear around that animal, as well as any other dogs resembling it.

Shelter dogs often exhibit fear-aggressive tendencies, due to their possibly dubious history. Your shelter dog could have been removed from the litter at three weeks of age or been savagely attacked by a person or animal. Or she might have been a stray for much of her life, having to deal with many harrowing experiences on a daily basis. These types of situations often cause the rescued shelter dog to be, at the very least, reserved and, at the worst, profoundly fearful of anything even remotely threatening.

Food aggression occurs in part because of the strength of the canine food drive. The hunger drive of wild canines has been largely retained by domestic dogs, even though plenty of food is readily available to them on a daily basis.

A dog will show food aggression under several circumstances. If your dog has spent part of his life as a stray, odds are he had to learn to fight for his meals. Bring a stray dog into your home, then, and you might find that he trounces on your other dog at dinner time, completely bullying the dog and hogging the food dish. Shelter dogs often have the same mind-set; many of them came from the streets or from unappreciative homes, where food might not have been provided regularly.

Food aggression can also occur because of dominance issues. If one dog is clearly dominant over another, chances are that the two won't exhibit much food aggression at all, once an initial confrontation has occurred. The problem comes when you own two dogs who are very close in stature and have not yet been able to resolve the dominance issue. Food becomes a great bone of contention between them. Dinnertime becomes a struggle to dominate, rather than an enjoyable experience. One dog will growl or nip at the other, who then returns the favor. Often it can escalate to a full-out battle, with possible injury to both pets.

Less frequently, a real bully of a dog might exert dominance over a less domineering pet at dinnertime and not know when to stop the intimidation. The attacked dog becomes frightened and goes into fear mode, assuming a defensive posture. One dog is fighting due to an inflated sense of importance, while the other is fighting out of terror. A nasty scene can ensue.

Your dominant dog can also show aggression toward you, or toward another member of the family if the person attempts to handle the food bowl while the dog is eating. In his mind, he is the dominant leader and has every right in the world to eat in peace, without any interruptions from you or anyone else. If a human (whom he considers a subordinate) actually has the nerve to try to take his food away while he is eating it, that "subordinate" is going to be disciplined, usually with a growl and a quick nip, but sometimes with a serious bite.

This mind-set in a dog is a serious problem and can result in upsetting injury, often to those who least expect it, such as a small child. In fact, far more children are bitten by dogs each year than adults, because of their initial ignorance of danger. Offending dogs who bite a child for coming too close to his food bowl don't think they are doing anything wrong but are in their minds simply disciplining a lesser member of the pack.

The problem stems from dogs' believe they are dominant over the humans in the family. Most times, that mistaken conception is caused by the owner's ignorance of canine psychology and a complete lack of leadership. Spoil your dog, allow him to sleep in bed with you, let him beg for scraps or win at games of strength or speed, and you, too, will help create a dominant little bully, one very capable of showing food-aggressive tendencies.

Hereditary aggression is preprogrammed into a dog. The problem can be difficult to predict and will often not surface until the dog enters adolescence. Other dogs, however, can show abnormal aggressive behavior right from puppyhood. Dogs with a genetic predisposition toward aggression will act in very unpredictable ways; sometimes they will be friendly and affectionate while at other times act as if possessed by a demon, growling at or biting other pets or humans with no apparent provocation. Owners of these pets often lead very stressful lives, trying on one hand to prevent injury to themselves or other loved ones, while on the other hand dreading the thought of perhaps needing to have the dog euthanized.

No outside stimuli can cause the problem, though certain situations can trigger aggressive outbursts. A stranger walking too close to the dog, a child innocently trying to pet her, or even an unexpected noise can all set off your dog if she has this problem. Again, the root cause of hereditary aggression is biological, not environmental, and not much can be done to eliminate the fault.

Maternal aggression can occur whenever someone or something comes too close to a mother dog's litter, particularly when the puppies are newborns. The aggression might even be directed at you, the owner, if the dog feels you are taking too many liberties with her litter. She may growl or nip or even bite until you (or whomever she deems a threat) retreat to a "safe" distance. Though more common in cats, maternal aggression can and does occur often enough in dogs to make it an issue.

Maternal aggression in domestic dogs is unpredictable. Some canine mothers will become agitated and worried upon a human being's approach (perhaps even yours), while others don't seem to care at all. A stray female, often preoccupied with her own survival, might even abandon her litter in order to ensure her own survival.

The timid, reserved female dog can often exhibit the most maternal aggression, due to her innate feelings of insecurity. Her instinctive desire to flee a potentially stressful situation clashes with her desire to protect her babies; this can result in profound aggression toward the "invading" individual.

Most canine mothers have a good sense of who is and who isn't a threat to their puppies, however. As most owners are seen as benevolent leaders by their dogs, a nursing mother will normally allow her owner contact with the litter, out of pack respect. Let a dog or another cat get too close to her, however, and that same sweet female will probably not be very amused.

Dogs exhibiting high levels of *prey aggression* will not be trustworthy around cats, other small pets (including toy dog breeds), and various small wild animals. They will find the presence of the animal to be stimulating in a predatory sense and may attempt to stalk and kill it. Often territorial aggression and prey aggression are difficult to distinguish; prey aggression is usually directed at a small animal and many times ends in death of the victim. Also, very little posturing or vocalization occurs during a predatory event, compared to territorial aggression, which normally involves barking, growling, snarling, and raised hackles, with most of the action being merely ritualistic in nature and little serious injury normally occurring.

Whether neutered or not, both males and females will exhibit some level of predatory drive at some time. Unneutered dogs will exhibit prey aggression more keenly, however, as will dogs who spend much of their lives outdoors. Stuck in a dog run or backyard all day, a dog will regularly see birds, squirrels, mice, cats, and other small animals scurry by, perhaps just out of reach. These regular "teasing" events will only serve to reinforce and accentuate any predatory instincts present in your dog. The other animals are almost within reach, but not quite, causing your dog to want them all the more.

Play aggression occurs in puppies and adolescent dogs. During the first few months of life, puppies learn to stalk, coordinate attacks, and socialize, primarily through playing with their littermates. They will take turns sneaking up on and wrestling with each other whenever possible. They also learn to work out their dominance hierarchy through these physical play sessions, the boldest and strongest becoming the most dominant, with the weakest and least expressive becoming the most subordinate.

Your dog might continue to exhibit this playful stalking and roughhousing behavior with you, a family member, or a visitor if she is encouraged to do so. Rarely does actual harm comes to the "victim"; it is just a game that the "attacker" has loved to play since puppyhood. The puppy, young dog, or adult pet might jump on you, then playfully nip at you. After the mock attack, the aggressor dog usually is as friendly as can be.

Some dogs never learn what behavior is acceptable and

what is not, primarily because their owners never teach them. You may take a puppy from her littermates (whom she has been aggressively playing with for weeks) and then shower her with love and attention without realizing that the puppy needs behavioral guidance right from the start in order to learn what is appropriate behavior. If you do not give the little pooch clearly defined dos and don'ts, she simply continues to behave as she did with her brothers and sisters. She will play-bite, jump, stalk, and wrestle with you until taught otherwise. If not addressed, this obnoxious behavior will follow the dog into adulthood.

Redirected aggression is common in all animals. Have you ever tried to mediate an argument between two friends only to have them both attack you? Or have you ever gotten so angry over something that you ended up taking out your frustrations on another person, even though he or she might have had nothing to do with it? These are perfect examples of redirected aggression. You can't do anything about the problem itself, so you simply vent your anger on the nearest vulnerable victim.

Dogs, like humans, are very capable of this. For instance, have you ever tried to break up a dog fight? If so, you may have had one or both of the dogs actually attack you instead of each other. That's redirected aggression. Both know that you are an easy, harmless target for their tensions and fears; attacking you is a way to release these fears, without losing face.

If you have been the victim of redirected canine aggression, odds are you were simply at the wrong place at the wrong time, such as in the middle of a dog fight or at the veterinarian's clinic trying to hold your frightened dog still for a vaccination.

SOLUTIONS

To minimize *dominance/territorial aggression* in your dog, you should:

1. Have your dog neutered before six months of age. Whether your pet is a male or female, allowing him or her to remain unneutered will only encourage dominance/territorial disputes, as well as create tension between you and the pet over issues of excessive marking and disobedience. Neutering (castrating a male or spaying a female) will remove sexual tensions from the mix and make it possible for two or more dogs of the same gender to live side by side in relative harmony.

2. Prevent your dog from having unsupervised access to the outdoors, which will nearly guarantee that he will eventually get into fights with other animals, causing him to gradually view other dogs as dangerous and threatening, instead of playful and fun.

3. Do your best to keep your dog's home environment as calm and predictable as possible, to avoid the chance of his experiencing any traumatic episodes, such as a group of small children suddenly chasing him around the house or the neighbor's Doberman rushing in to say hi. Ensure that your dog is not presented with a situation in which he must defend his territory or exert his dominance over strange invaders. Never allow anyone to play too roughly with him, especially young children, who often do not know where to draw the line.

4. Socialize your dog from as early on as possible. Allow him to be around different adults and responsible children right from the beginning, as well as any other dogs you may have in the home (provided they are not aggressive themselves). Take him for walks down busy streets as soon as he is old enough (never before his eleventh week). Let willing strangers pet and stroke him

and give him treats that you supply. Introducing a kitten into a dog's world can be successful but should be attempted only if the dog in question is a puppy, or has had successful cat relationships in the past. Trying to introduce an adult cat into your dog's world might not work out well unless the cat in question has had positive relationships with dogs in the past.

5. If you decide to obtain another dog, consider introducing the newcomer to your established dog away from your home at first, perhaps at a neighbor's house, the breeder's facility, or the shelter. Your established dog sees your home as his territory and may be quite protective of it, especially toward another adult dog. Allowing them to meet on neutral turf is a good way to avoid this territorial conflict. Once home, do not allow the new dog to eat out of the established dog's dish or rest in his favorite spots. Respect the established dog's status, and let him know you consider him higher in the pack hierarchy than the new pooch. Allow the dogs to work out their own relationship; though it may actually involve some growling and nipping, it shouldn't turn into anything serious. Nonetheless, observe them carefully, and always support the dominant dog's position. For example, if the new dog gets growled at for eating from the established dog's dish, do not punish the established dog for this behavior. He was right for growling at the upstart, who had no business sticking his nose in where it didn't belong.

6. If adopting an adult dog, be sure to first observe his behavior closely before taking him home. Is he in with other dogs or by himself? Does he have any scars on his body? Is he friendly and open to physical contact or sullen and cautious?

Offer him a toy or treat, then take it away, watching for his reaction. If he shows any possessiveness, move on to a different dog.

7. When choosing a puppy, opt for one who seems to interact with his littermates in a reasonable fashion. Avoid overly dominant, pushy puppies who seem to bully the others, as well as the puppies who shrink away from any confrontation. Pick one who shows curiosity yet knows when to back off. Also, make sure not to separate your puppy from his mother and littermates before his eighth week, to ensure he gets the proper maternal care, as well as the right amount of early socialization with his siblings.

8. Be the best leader you can be, to prevent your dog from feeling that he has to take on the reins of power. Ways to establish yourself as the leader include:

◆ Forbidding your dog from sleeping in bed with you, which teaches him that he has equal status with you.

◆ Feeding him only after you and the family have eaten. Leaders eat first; by allowing him to eat before you, you tell him that he is higher up in the pack than you.

◆ Making sure that you go through doors before he does. Leaders always go first; letting him always blow through a door before you teaches him he has more authority than you.

◆ Teaching him not to pull on the leash during a walk. Dogs who do so are expressing their dominance over you, as leaders always *lead*. Instead, teach him to walk by your side, on a loose leash.

◆ Taking control of greeting other persons and dogs. The leader always greets others before any other member of the pack. Allowing your dog to do this teaches him that he is top dog. Make sure that you do all the initial greetings from now on.

◆ Never allowing your dog to win at a "keep away" game or tug-of-war, which teaches him that he has physical power over you and that he can possess anything he wants without you being able to do anything about it. If he steals items of clothing from you and then refuses to give them back, keep a long leash on him in the home and use it to catch him. Then simply banish him to a bathroom or a travel crate for an hour or so, to let him know that his behavior was not acceptable and that you are in ultimate control.

9. Avoid keeping your dog in a front or back-yard for long periods of time, especially if he can see people and/or other animals walking by on a regular basis. Here is what happens: First, he sees someone walking by the yard. As the person approaches, your dog begins to bark, feeling as if his territory is being "invaded." He cannot confront the intruder, however, because of the fence. Without it, he would most likely approach the person and quickly realize that he or she is no threat. With the fence there, however, he cannot do so. He can only bark and worry. Then the person passes and begins walking away, making your dog think that his territorial display actually succeeded in

driving the "invader" away. Repeated many times each day, this scenario teaches the dog to be wary of strangers and to bark and carry on until they depart from his territory. After a few years of this, the dog begins to despise passersby; if accidentally let out, he could become aggressive. Instead of keeping your dog in the yard all day, consider keeping him in the home instead. After all, that's where all your valuables are anyway; if you are going to own a dog in part for theft deterrence, why not keep him inside, where all your belongings are? Most dogs should be able to go eight to nine hours without being let out to eliminate. If yours cannot, consider having a friendly neighbor come over to let the pooch out once or twice during the day. Keeping him in the home during the day will minimize the chances of his being constantly confronted by persons or other dogs, as would happen if he were to be in the yard all day (unless, of course, you keep all the curtains and blinds wide open).

10. Keep your dog in a travel crate while in your car. This will prevent him from seeing all of the activity going on around him and help to minimize the "fishbowl" feeling that dogs can develop in cars. Odds are doing so will substantially reduce his concerns about territorial encroachments while you are in the store shopping.

Eliminating *fear aggression* in a dog is a difficult task. As the root causes are often deeply ingrained or genetically determined, chances are the profoundly fear-aggressive dog will remain so. That said, several steps can be taken to prevent or reduce the occurrence of fear-aggressive episodes. If you know your dog has a tendency toward fear aggression, you should:

◆ Avoid putting her into confrontational circumstances. For instance, hosting a party with twenty three-year-olds as the guests is not a good idea. Also, do not force her to be petted by strangers, especially when she is showing clear signs of distress. Instead, allow her to initiate contact with someone, who can then give her a treat and a gentle pat on the chest. Instruct him or her not to pet the dog on the head, unless she seems to enjoy it, as fear-aggressive dogs will often panic upon being touched in and around the face. When having guests over the home, have them drop a few treats at their feet and allow the dog to come over for them. Then additional treats can be offered. If the dog seems willing, then guests can gently pet her while talking softly.

◆ Avoid loud or unexpected noises in the home, if possible, as they could panic the timid, fearful dog and cause her to bite if approached.

◆ Tell children and adults not to chase the dog or attempt to surprise her in any way.

◆ Consult with your veterinarian, who may be able to prescribe medication that will help the dog relax.

◆ Attempt to slowly desensitize her to stimuli that normally make her uneasy. If, for example, strangers make her worry, try taking a friend along on walks, making sure that the friend first walks on your right, with the dog on your left. Don't require the dog to interact with your friend at first; simply get her to accept the

person's presence. Every so often, have the
friend toss a treat onto the ground near the dog.
After a few sessions like this, quietly pass the
leash over to your friend, then change positions
for a few minutes. Continue to walk briskly,
with the friend avoiding any physical contact
with the dog. However, continue having the
friend drop a treat or two down on the ground.
Eventually, you can instruct the friend to give
the dog some basic commands, such as *sit* and
down. In this way, your dog will learn to
tolerate your friend's presence, and that strangers
aren't necessarily threatening. If she shows a
fear of strangers in the home, have friends come
over at the dog's dinner time, and allow them to
prepare the dog's meal, then place the dish
down on the floor. If this is done on a regular
basis, she will learn that strangers mean good
food is on the way.

To prevent fear aggression, try the following preventive
steps:

◆ Choose a puppy carefully. Never buy a pet from
a pet store or "backyard breeder," as these
venues rarely produce quality pets. Also, do not
take a puppy from any breeder who is willing to
let the dog go before her eighth week of life.
Also, look for a breeder who prefers to socialize
the puppies with humans from two weeks of age
and on. If adopting a puppy or dog from a
shelter, choose one who appears confident,
friendly, and curious around people and other
dogs. If the animal shows any timidity or fear,
keep looking.
◆ Try to set up a quiet, predictable environment
for your new pet, so that she can acclimate to

her new surroundings with as little worry as possible.

◆ Socialize the new puppy as much as possible, as soon as possible.

◆ Make sure not to allow anything shocking or potentially frightening to occur in your puppy's life from her eighth through her eleventh week of life. This period is known as the *fear imprint stage,* a well-documented period of psychological development during which a puppy is extremely vulnerable to fear-inducing stimuli. This stage exists as a self-preservation mechanism by which puppies in the wild, at first insatiably curious about their environments, learn to fear dangerous, unknown elements in their environment. The fear imprint stage helps keep them alive and close to Mom. In the domestic dog, however, it serves very little purpose other than to cause irrational fears to develop. By keeping the eight-to-eleven-week-old puppy away from potentially loud or shocking stimuli, you will help prevent irrational fears from developing, fears that could lead to aggression.

Ending *food aggression* that flares up between two dogs at dinnertime depends in part on how bad it has gotten. If the aggressor tends to only growl or nip at the victim a few times, you may be able to solve the problem by simply moving the dogs to opposite sides of the kitchen. Purchase an extra food and water dish and set each dog up in his own corner. This solution will work with dogs who simply do not feel comfortable having another pet so close by during feeding time.

This will probably not work with a dog who actively seeks to eat the other dog's food. This type of pushy canine wants to make a real statement to the other dog and will do so in part by eating his food. If this is the case in your home, the easiest solution is to simply feed each pet in a separate room. By doing so, you will relieve the stress that the victim has been experiencing, letting him eat in peace. You will also be halting the aggressive behavior of the dominant animal, an important factor, as allowing the behavior to continue only serves to reinforce it.

This solution will work better than punishing the offending dog, as doing so could actually escalate the problem. Whenever possible, it is better to remove the cause of the offensive behavior than to attempt to modify the actions of the offending dog. If separating them at dinnertime solves the problem, then so be it.

If food aggression is occurring between a dog and cat, separation should also take place. As your cat is easily able to jump up to a counter several feet above the floor, consider simply feeding him atop a kitchen counter while the dog eats undisturbed below.

If your dog is showing food-aggressive tendencies toward you or someone else in your family, that is a different matter. At no time should a dog be allowed to growl at, nip, or bite a human, regardless of age. In addition to following any advice given here, the owner of an aggressive dog should also contact an experienced canine behaviorist as soon as possible, in order to solve the problem and prevent dire injury.

That said, it is important to respect the pet's need and desire to eat in peace. Children should not be allowed to stick their fingers into your dog's food bowl while he is eating or tease the pet by picking up the bowl and moving it around. Consider not allowing toddlers into the kitchen at all while your dog eats, to prevent any potential problems. As far as you are concerned, though you should allow your pooch to eat in peace, you should nevertheless have the right to pick up the dog's bowl if necessary. Your dog should never have the right to tell you not to do so.

If your dog growls at you whenever you attempt to touch his bowl, try this. First, before feeding him, clip his leash on. Next, place his dinner down and let him eat for a minute or so. Then, pick up his leash and command him to "sit" (hopefully you have taught him this basic command). Praise him, then pick up the bowl and place a treat into it. Make sure he sees you do this. Then put the bowl down again and say, "OK!" in a happy tone. Your dog will rejoice at finding the treat. Repeat this at least once or twice during every dinner. Eventually, you will be able to simply pick up his bowl whenever you want, as he will think it a prelude to a yummy treat. All thoughts of guarding the food will be gone, replaced by the anticipation of better things to come.

In more severe cases of food aggression, you may have to forgo feeding your dog from a bowl on the floor completely and actually feed him his nightly meal by hand, one palmful at a time. Though this will be time-consuming, it is an effective way of putting a stop to the aggressive behavior. The reason it works is simple: there is no longer a bowl for the dog to guard. All the food comes from your hand. To use this method, first measure out the normal amount of dog food into a container (not the dog's normal bowl) and place it up on a counter, close enough for you to reach, but high enough so that he cannot get to it. Then sit down and call the dog over. Begin feeding him one handful at a time from the container, making sure that he sits each time for it. From now on, he must earn his food. Continue to feed him in this way until the food is gone. Use this method for one week. Then, place his empty food bowl down on the floor again, and, instead of letting him eat out of your hand, pick up the bowl, place a handful of food into it, then put it down for him to eat. Repeat this until all the food has been eaten. For this stage, you needn't make him sit each time. What eventually happens is that he begins to associate you handling the bowl with him receiving food. Do this for at least two weeks.

The last step is to place his bowl down, put about one-quarter of his food into it, then allow him to eat it. Then, pick the bowl up, put the next quarter-serving in it, then place it back down. Continue doing this until the food is gone. Slowly increase the amount you put into the bowl each time until he is back to eating all of it at one time. However, continue to pick the bowl up at random times to place a tasty treat into it while food is still remaining. Do so for the rest of the dog's life.

The first step in dealing with *hereditary aggression* is taking your dog to your veterinarian, who will help you determine if, in fact, she does have a genetic predisposition toward aggression. Sometimes hereditary aggression can be mistaken for fear aggression; your veterinarian will help you make that determination. The root of the problem may also be a medical one; if this is the case, there may be a chance to minimize the problem. For instance, an injured or sick dog might be exhibiting unpredictable aggressive tendencies because of great pain; because of the species's stoic nature, you might ever be aware of the problem. Ending the pain could cure the aggression.

If, however, your dog is deemed to be genetically predisposed to aggression, there can be very little success in attempting to successfully modify her violent, unpredictable behavior. Short of finding a Good Samaritan willing to care for the pet, few options save euthanization exist.

Some veterinarians have experienced varying levels of success, however, by using tranquilizers and mood-altering drugs to minimize the dangerous behavior. Just as Lithium, Prozac, Xanax, and Valium are used to modulate aberrant human behaviors, so can similar medications be used on dogs. Consult your veterinarian on this before taking any further steps. The right medication just might reduce the pet's aggressive episodes enough to allow nearly normal relationships to commence, perhaps for the first time.

Maternal aggression in canines tends to subside on its own, after a few weeks. Brought on by hormonal changes initiated by birthing and nursing, these changes begin to subside as the puppies get closer and closer to being weaned. If your dog has just given birth and is exhibiting signs of maternal aggression, do not attempt to modify the behavior or punish her; just let nature take its course. Within a few weeks, all should be back to normal. She should allow you access to the puppies within a week or two of birth, so just be patient. While she is away eating or eliminating, you can certainly handle the puppies; just be sure to wash your hands thoroughly before doing so, for the sake of the litter's health.

The best way to avoid maternal aggression in your dog is to have her spayed before she becomes sexually mature. If you insist on breeding your dog (something best left to professionals), be sure to provide her with a quiet, warm, secure nesting area. If she seems to be just as affectionate and relaxed as usual, then it will probably be OK to interact with the babies. If you doubt her mood, however, back off and let her be.

Prey aggression can be minimized in a number of ways. First, have your dog neutered. Doing so will reduce her level of prey drive and help keep her mind off her predatory urges.

Next, don't allow your dog to roam the neighborhood. If you do, she will have a much higher chance of her predatory instincts being turned on by the birds, mice, squirrels, rats, moles, snakes, baby raccoons, or skunks she encounters.

In the home, consider not having rodents, birds, rabbits, ferrets, or small reptiles as pets. If you must have them, be sure to locate them in an area of the home that your dog cannot access on her own. Place a secure lid on all small pet habitats, to prevent a curious snout or paw from delving in. Be sure, however, that the cover has an adequate number of breathing holes in it.

If you bring a puppy into the home, it is possible to teach her to interact with a kitten on a friendly basis. In fact, many dogs and cats become fast friends when raised together. If you are getting a puppy and think a cat might also be in your future, consider getting the kitten at the same time and allowing them to interact regularly. Do not attempt to bring a puppy into the realm of an established cat, however, as the cat will rarely accept her. Bringing a kitten into the world of an established dog can be done, provided the dog in question has a sweet disposition, and has had positive experiences with cats in the past, perhaps spending puppyhood with a cat or kitten. Whenever your dog interacts with your cat, praise her lavishly, but avoid involving treat rewards, as the presence of food could provoke a possessive response, directed at the cat. Instead, simply use physical and vocal praise.

Play aggression isn't aggression at all, at least not in the strictest sense. Your dog isn't serious; it's just a game and a way to exert his status. Nonetheless, the behavior can be annoying to yourself and other persons, who might not appreciate having a dog suddenly play-bite them.

To discourage your dog from play-attacking or biting persons in the home, you can try a number of techniques. First, as close to the time of the "attack" as possible, clap your hands together briskly and say, "No!" in a fairly stern tone. Don't hit the dog or scream at the top of you lungs. Or try placing soda cans with twenty small pebbles or coins inside around the home, so that one is always close at hand. As soon as the dog begins to act too roughly, pick up a can and throw it onto the floor near the pet, while simultaneously saying, "No!" The raucous sound of the items inside of the can should sober the dog right up and halt the unwanted behavior. Also, try using a water pistol or plant sprayer bottle filled with water and a teaspoon of white vinegar. Just as he begins to play-bite or roughhouse, spray him in the mouth with the pistol or sprayer bottle. Getting a face full of vinegar water once or twice should be enough to eliminate the behavior. Remember not to lose your cool;

after all, he thinks it's a game and needs to be taught that you just don't want to play in that fashion.

Take your dog to an obedience class, where both of you will learn how to interact with each other and where you will learn to efficiently control him. Also, read as many books on canine behavior as you can to truly understand where he is coming from. Once he learns to regularly obey and respect you, his naughty play-biting and roughhousing should cease.

The best way to minimize *redirected aggression* in your dog is to first do all you can to prevent it from happening. Be sure not to interfere during or right after any profoundly stressful event has occurred. If your dog is having a fight with another animal, for example, do not attempt to separate them physically. Instead, throw a bucket of cold water on them both, to distract them out of the conflict. If your dog has just undergone a traumatic experience and is still petrified, don't pick her up. Instead, call her over to you, or else give her a few minutes to calm down before trying to comfort her. If she comes to you when called, it means she is thinking rationally and probably won't show any redirected aggression, unless she has serious, painful injuries.

If she is injured and in need of immediate care, however, you may not be able to avoid some level of redirected aggression. Remember that you must not correct the dog for this; she is highly stressed and is only reacting according to instinct. Approach her calmly and talk to her; try to access her state of mind. If she seems calm enough and responsive to you, go ahead and transport her to the veterinarian. If she appears to be in shock, however, you may have to resort to throwing a towel or blanket over her before attempting to lift her up. If you suspect that she might have spinal cord damage, do nothing until you have spoken to your veterinarian or an emergency pet clinician.

To help prevent redirected aggression, make sure to:

- Neuter your dog to reduce the chances of a fight occurring.
- Socialize her from an early age.
- Handle her as much as possible, including looking in her mouth and at her feet.
- Limit her access to potentially aggressive or dangerous animals. If taking her to a dog park, try to evaluate the other dogs present before allowing yours to join in.
- Make sure her environment is safe and secure to prevent stress and injury.
- Do not allow her to roam outdoors. When walking her, use a leash, especially in high-traffic areas.
- Don't lose your temper or try to modify redirected aggression, as it is a nonthinking, instinctive reaction to pain or fear.

ANTISOCIAL BEHAVIOR

DESCRIPTION

Any dog who shies away from the company of humans or other dogs is thought of as being antisocial. Antisocial behavior taken to the extreme will inevitably become fear aggression; here we are differentiating between the two by establishing the reaction to the circumstances. A cautious dog who chooses to run away and hide is being antisocial. A timid, frightened dog who turns to fight is being fear-aggressive.

Any dog who shies away from being touched is showing some antisocial tendencies. Those who disappear whenever guests come over are exhibiting a higher level of antisocial behavior, while those dogs who refuse to allow their owners to touch them or even occupy the same room are suffering from an even higher level of antisocial tendencies.

WHY YOUR DOG IS DOING THIS

Everyone wants their dogs to be as sociable as possible. Normally they are, as dogs are among the most social of creatures. Unfortunately, this is not always the case, because of either the inherent personality traits of the dog, the behavioral limitations of the breed, or the dog's history. A dog might simply have a shy temperament or belong to a breed (such as the Afghan, chowchow, or Lhasa Apso) that doesn't enjoy uninvited company. Or your dog might prefer to spend time alone due to a bad experience in his past, such as repeated physical abuse from a previous owner or another pet. Whatever the reason, some dogs just won't want to be as sociable as you'd like them to be.

You should expect your dog to show a desire to be with you and the persons he regularly interacts with, however. If he doesn't, something is indeed amiss and should be addressed. He should also at least tolerate guests in the home, particularly those who visit on a regular basis. Don't ask him to quickly warm up to a total stranger, though, particularly one of large stature or someone with a boisterous nature. Young children can often be hard for some dogs to feel comfortable with, unless they act calmly and quietly, without lots of unpredictable motion. Toy breeds can be especially cautious around strangers, due in large part to their diminutive stature. If you were only eleven inches high, you'd be cautious around strange two-legged giants, too!

SOLUTION

If your dog shows timidity around other persons or animals, the first thing to do is not force the issue. Don't allow anyone to chase the dog and pick him up. Instead, let the dog decide if and when he will come over and greet the visitor. You can help him along, though, by first showing him that you have no fear of the visitor and enjoy him or her enough to hug. You can also allow the visitor to place a tasty treat on the floor near where he or she is sitting, in hopes that the dog will eventually come out and eat it. If you do this each time a guest comes over, the dog will eventually be conditioned to see the presence of a stranger as a good thing.

If children come over, instruct them not to chase the dog, yell, scream, or run around the home. Have them act just as an adult would, quietly and calmly. Use the same treat conditioning exercise each time, to teach your dog that kids aren't all that bad. When he finally does warm up to the child, make sure that he or she is as gentle as possible. Don't expect your reserved dog to be comfortable with toddlers, though, as they tend to be very grabby and might end up pinching the dog's skin or pulling on his tail or ears.

Antisocial behavior toward other dogs will usually work itself out over time. The timid or cautious dog will eventually have no choice but to accept the presence of the more outgoing animal if, in fact, this extrovert is going to be around on a regular basis. Try not to interfere unless the behavior erupts into violence. To avoid this, make sure to always introduce a new dog to the established one on neutral turf, away from the home.

If you have just adopted a new dog who seems to be avoiding you, give him some time. Even the most timid dog will eventually come around and learn to trust his owner, provided he or she is calm, patient, and gentle. Speak softly to your new dog, offer him treats, and never initiate contact. Wait for him to come to you. He will eventually do so, inviting you to pet him. By not forcing the issue, you will allow the dog to develop trust in you, the cornerstone to minimizing antisocial behavior. Remove doubt and fear, and the dog will yearn for your touch.

BAD BREATH

DESCRIPTION

Though this sounds humorous, bad breath can and often does occur in dogs. Any foul or sour smell coming from your dog's mouth can indicate a potentially serious health problem in the making.

WHY YOUR DOG IS DOING THIS

Though obviously not a behavioral problem, canine bad breath can be indicative of a physiological disorder in the making. The first suspect should always be a health problem in the dog's mouth. Bacterial buildup, tartar, plaque, or food lodged between teeth can cause your dog to develop bad breath. Gum disease, abscesses, or oral tumors might also be responsible for a bad odor.

Bad oral odor in your dog could also be caused by a disorder in the pet's gastrointestinal tract. Infection, ulcers, tumors, or severe allergic reaction to a certain food could also be the culprit. Or the food he eats might simply be too odoriferous for your taste. Your dog might even be getting into the garbage without your knowing it.

SOLUTION

The first step to take is to bring your dog to the veterinarian, who will perform a thorough exam to establish the cause. Odds are he or she will want to clean your dog's teeth. If so, allow the procedure, as it will most likely cure the problem, while extending the life of your dog's teeth at the same time. Your veterinarian will also be able to spot a more serious physiological problem and may even recommend a different, less odor-producing food. If your dog is over ten years of age, however, you may want to think twice about having him anesthetized, a procedure almost always required for teeth cleaning. Old dogs, as well as toy breeds, have a higher risk of reacting poorly to this procedure, so consult closely with your veterinarian before allowing it.

Keeping your dog's teeth clean will go a long way in preventing bad breath and tooth decay. Brushing a dog's teeth isn't normally an easy task, however; most adult canines don't take too kindly to it. If you start your puppy out from the beginning, however, you may be able to brush his teeth once a week or so without much objection, provided you do so quickly and painlessly. Your veterinarian can provide you with the proper toothpaste and brush. Start out by gently massaging the young puppy's gums, and slowly progress to lightly brushing the teeth with a soft-bristle brush and some vet-approved toothpaste. Don't use human toothpaste, as it can irritate the canine mouth. If you have any problem at all, however, don't continue, as you might cause your dog to distrust you. Let the veterinarian do it instead. You can try brushing your adult dog's teeth using the same method. If he resists strongly, however, defer to your veterinarian, who can anesthetize the dog and do a thorough cleaning.

BARKING

DESCRIPTION

Along with house-training mishaps and biting, unwanted barking is probably the most irritating and common behavioral problem dog owners complain about. The dog in question will bark incessantly (particularly when the owners are not home), prompting neighbors to complain. Owners of these noisy hounds often receive warnings or summons from the local authorities or even eviction notices from irate landlords. These delinquent dogs cause many sleepless nights and countless frayed nerves.

The dog who barks too much does so under different circumstances. Guests knocking on the door, a person walking by the home, or an unexpected sound can all trigger the barking, which can last for seconds, minutes, or hours. The homebound dog might bark continuously from loneliness or boredom; the spoiled dog might bark when desiring attention or food. Whatever the reason, incessant barking can drive an owner crazy and cause him or her to ultimately hand the dog over to a shelter.

WHY YOUR DOG IS DOING THIS

Barking is a normal instinct for a domestic dog. A tool for communication, the bark is often used as a warning sign to other pack members that a potential intruder is close by. Indeed, many persons own dogs is for this very reason; no home security system works better than the finely tuned ears and noses of watchful canines, who then alert others of the danger by yelping their fuzzy little heads off. Interestingly, this instinct is not nearly as well developed in wild canines, who tend not to bark much at all but instead either keep quiet or howl to communicate. Over the centuries, the barking trait has actually been encouraged by humans, primarily as an intruder alert system.

Unfortunately, we now live in much denser surroundings than did people of decades ago. This serves to make excessive barking a real nuisance. The close proximity of people only serves to set off the barking instinct even more, often resulting in haggard, angry neighbors.

In addition to warning other "pack" members of a potential territorial breach, barking can also be the result of a dog becoming overly excited about something, such as the expectation of a meal or a walk. Some dogs will bark while alone in the home, due to a feeling of loneliness or separation anxiety, while others bark from sheer boredom.

Overly spoiled dogs will use barking as a means of controlling their owners. *Bark, bark, bark! I want that piece of cookie in your hand! Bark! Pet me! Bark! Let me up into your lap!* Some dominant dogs will continue to bark at a visitor even after the person has calmly sat down and the owner has welcomed him or her into the home and pleaded for the dog to be quiet. Desperate, many hapless owners will yell and scream at this point, which only serves to increase the barking, as most dogs see the vocalizations of the owners as just more barking by a pack member. They happily join in, causing the owners to yell even louder. This cascading cycle never succeeds in shutting the noisy pooch up.

Dogs might also bark incessantly if they are nervous, timid, fearful pets, constantly worrying about things. These dogs bark as a way to release pent-up anxiety. A form of redirected aggression, this type of barking is very difficult to stop.

SOLUTION

The best way to minimize barking is to train your dog from puppyhood to look forward to people coming to the door and entering the home. Though this negates somewhat the benefit of having your dog warn you of a possible intruder, the advantages of not having to hear the constant racket may be a more valuable commodity to you. Plus, if someone tries to break into your home in the middle of the night, your dog will know to bark, even if he has been conditioned not to do so during the day, when you are home. He will sense the difference, as well as your heightened concern.

To teach your puppy that people coming to the door is no big deal, begin desensitizing him to the sound of knocking on the door, as well as the doorbell (if you have one).

First, with the puppy on a leash next to you, casually and happily rap your knuckles on the wall or a desk a few times, then immediately give him a small treat while simultaneously praising him. Do this all over the home, randomly, about six or eight times. Then repeat it again, several times throughout the day. After a few days, take the puppy over to the front door and perform the knocking/praising exercise there. Do it several times, then repeat the exercise three or four more times each day. After a week of this, step out of your home (with the puppy still inside), close the door, knock on it, then step in and immediately give him a treat and praise. Repeat this randomly throughout the day, and continue working on this for at least a week. Your puppy should by this time begin to associate any knocking sounds with yummy treats. Then, with you and the puppy inside, have a friend knock on the door. As soon as the puppy hears it, give him a treat and praise. Then have the friend come in and praise the dog as well. Make it a real happy greeting time for the pooch.

Desensitize him to the doorbell as well. To do so, take him outside the home to the front door. Ring the bell, then give him a treat and praise. Repeat this randomly throughout the day for a week or so. Then have the same friend ring the bell with you and the dog inside. Immediately upon hearing the bell, give the puppy a treat and praise him. Repeat this until the sound of the bell becomes a happy, expectant event for him.

If your adult dog already has a barking problem while you are home with him, here is what to do. You need to find a way to turn the behavior on and off at will by using vocal commands. In this way, you will gain some control over it and also teach the dog to pay attention to you even when someone is outside the home. First, clip his leash onto his collar. Next, have a friend come up to the front door, who needn't knock, as the dog will sense his or her presence. With the dog in front of you, the moment he begins to bark, say, *"Bark! Bark!"* Then give him a treat and praise him. Try to anticipate exactly when he is going to bark, and give the *Bark!* command right at that moment. Eventually what you want to do is teach him to associate the barking with the verbal command, so that you can get him to bark whenever you want, even when no one is around. Practice this several times each day for a week. You will eventually succeed in putting a word to the behavior, the first step in controlling it.

Next, you need to come up with a way to stop the new behavior. With him on-leash, have him sit in front of you. Next, give him the *Bark!* command. Let him bark once or twice, then say, *"Quiet!"* in a commanding voice. As soon as he stops, give a treat and praise him. Continue to work this exercise, but gradually increase the time between when he stops barking and when he gets the treat. Eventually you will be able to quell the barking just by saying, *"Quiet!"* The final step is to have a friend walk up and knock on the door once, with your dog close by. Let him bark a few times, then say, in a commanding voice, *"Quiet!"* At that moment, also have a treat in your hand, ready to give the dog. His focus should switch from the knocking to you and the treat. After he has been quiet for a second or two, give him the treat and praise. Then let the friend in and have him or her also give the dog a treat. Continue to work this exercise until you can easily halt the barking with the *Quiet!* command. Also, begin mixing simple verbal praise with treat rewards, so that the dog gets a treat only every fourth or fifth time. You should always wean the dog off the treat reward as the behavior becomes solidified, so that he begins to perform for you and not the food. Give a treat every now and then, however, to keep him guessing.

If your dog barks incessantly when you are not home, the problem becomes more difficult. There are several methods you can try, however, to minimize the behavior. First, do not keep your dog in a fenced front yard. Doing so teaches him to bark vociferously, for a good reason. When in the yard, what does he see? He sees people and other dogs approaching the home, which, in most dogs, will engage a territorial reaction, causing him to bark. He is stimulated and slightly frustrated, due to the fence keeping him from actually investigating these "intruders" close up. Then what happens? The person (or dog) walks by, passes the home, and disappears down the street. Your dog thinks he has successfully scared them away. This acts as a self-reinforcing exercise for him. He thinks the barking worked to drive off the intruder, so he continues to do it whenever someone walks by. To avoid this, keep him in the home or in a dog run in a secluded section of the backyard, where he will not be continuously subjected to a procession of people and dogs.

If your barking dog is in the home, consider keeping him in an area of the home that does not afford him a perfect view of the front of the house, where he can see people and pets walking by and immediately begin barking. With you not there to correct the behavior, he will reinforce himself and continue to yelp his head off. Consider also closing the blinds and curtains or keeping him in a basement or family room where he does not have a window facing the street.

This next technique may sound unusual to you, but it works. First, teach your barking dog the *Bark!* and *Quiet!* commands, as mentioned earlier. Next, go out and purchase two inexpensive two-way radios, or walkie-talkies. You should be able to obtain a set in a toy store for less than forty dollars. Turn the volume up on one, and leave it hanging from the doorknob of the front door of your home. Then close the blinds or curtains and leave the home, taking the other radio with you. Walk far enough away from the home so that your dog cannot easily sense you but close enough so that you can hear if he is barking. Then, have a friend walk up, knock on the door once, and walk away quickly. When your dog begins to bark, give the *Quiet!* command into your radio, saying it several times as you walk back to the home. If all goes well, your dog should be surprised enough to stop barking long enough for you to go in and praise him. Work this several times a week, making sure to praise the dog lavishly if he halts his barking. Then, whenever you leave the home, hang the radio on the doorknob. Its presence should help keep your dog quiet. Be sure to work the exercise at least once or twice a week, indefinitely, to keep it fresh in his mind.

Some dogs will continue to bark when left at home alone, no matter what you do. This can cause all manner of problems with the neighbors or the landlord and could lead to a summons or eviction. For these dogs, the only alternative is the use of an approved bark collar, which delivers a mild electric shock whenever the dog barks. These are available in most pet shops, but it is highly recommended that you first meet with a trained canine behaviorist before going to this step. First, he or she will evaluate the situation and determine if, in fact, the collar is needed. Second, if it seems to be the only alternative, the behaviorist will be there to instruct you on the collar's use. Improperly operated, the collar can amplify the problem, so please do not take it upon yourself to use the collar without speaking to the expert first.

A dog who barks incessantly while in an automobile (either with you there or not) can be very hard to control. The reason for this is simple: an automobile is a territory in miniature, surrounded by glass. Dogs feel as if they are in a fishbowl; this causes them to feel more vulnerable to strangers walking by. They bark, see the people walk by, and think that they have scared the intruders away. The combination of feeling vulnerable and thinking that he has scared the intruders away from the car causes the problem to escalate. The only real way to deal with this problem is to keep your dog in a plastic travel crate while in the car. Doing so is the safest way of transporting him, as it prevents your dog from being jostled around or flung forward during an accident or sudden stop, and also stops him from interfering with your operation of the vehicle. If you must leave him in your car while going into a store, have him in the crate and place a towel or light blanket over it to block his view of people going by. Just be sure to crack a window open to let in fresh air. If the day is a particularly hot one, however, leave your dog home to prevent any chance of heatstroke. Also, if your dog's crate is too large to fit in your car, you may need to either leave him at home or else seriously consider obtaining a vehicle large enough for the crate to fit in.

The only way to stop your fearful dog from barking is by slowly desensitizing him to his fears. A first step in doing so is attending a local obedience class with him, in an attempt to improve your control of him (and his opinion of you). Fearful dogs often are so because of the owner not projecting any sense of leadership; such dogs feel rudderless but aren't quite up to taking over themselves. The result is a lack of confidence, leading to behavior problems, including barking. After you and your dog take the class (in which he will be able to socialize with people and other dogs), be sure to work on increasing his self-confidence by working his obedience and praising him lavishly for it. Also, allow him to socialize as much as possible, provided he does not display any fear-aggressive tendencies. Often all a dog like this needs is to make a few close friends outside of you and your immediate family.

Teaching your dog to perform a few tricks is another way to boost his self-esteem. Tricks are fun for all and don't involve negative reinforcement. Your dog learns to perform, use his head, and think rationally, all for praise and treats. To learn how to teach him a few tricks, visit your library or bookstore, which will both carry books on the subject. Once he learns to expand his repertoire of behaviors, his confidence will increase, helping to minimize barking derived from worry.

BATHING, AVERSION TO

DESCRIPTION

Most dogs aren't fond of being bathed. Some will struggle to get out of the tub, while others will just shake and bear it. A few might actually put up a real fight and attempt to bite at their "tormentor." All in all, it's not a very pretty scene.

WHY YOUR DOG IS DOING THIS

Like human children, most dogs seem to have a dislike for getting clean. The problem might have less to do with the actual cleaning procedure, though, and more to do with being physically restrained while at the same time being drenched with water or getting stinging soap in the eyes. Any dog who has been intimidated or manhandled during a bath or who has gotten soap in his or her eyes will probably put up a fuss during the procedure. Owners who bathe their dogs in the backyard using cold hose water will most likely have a reluctant dog on their hands.

SOLUTION

Dogs being dogs, there will definitely be times when you'll need to bathe yours. Playing at the park, romping in a muddy field, swimming, parasitic infestation, or contact with a messy, oily, or toxic substance will require a good washing. Unfortunately, if your dog is like most, he won't much care for being wetted down and lathered up. Many people therefore decide to make a monthly pilgrimage to the groomer, who will expertly wash and dry your pooch

and even trim his fur and nails, if need be. Going this route
can cost upward of thirty or forty dollars (depending on the
size and breed of your dog) but, for some, can be well
worth it.

For others, bathing their own dogs is not only cost-
efficient but also a good way to exercise a little leadership.
Being able to successfully bathe your dog means you definitely have control and also a substantial amount of leadership status in the eyes of your dog. A dog who
successfully and regularly escapes bathing is one who has
a real lack of respect for his owner. Odds are other areas
of the relationship need work as well.

If your dog dislikes being bathed, you will need to re-
condition him into thinking that a bath is actually a good
thing. Here's what to do:

1. At least once a day, clip a leash on your dog
   and bring him into the bathroom. Have him sit,
   them give him a few tasty treats. Or feed him
   his dinner in the bathroom each night for a few
   weeks. Doing so will begin to make the
   bathroom seem a friendlier, happier place to him.
2. After a few weeks, instead of having him sit on
   the floor of the bathroom, have him jump into
   the tub and sit. Then continue to give him treats,
   or feed him there in the tub, for at least a week.
   That's right; in the tub!
3. Next, bring him into the tub and give him a
   treat. With the dog standing and the end of the
   leash in your hand, pour warm water from a
   large plastic container onto your dog's back, all
   the while praising him. Then immediately give
   him several tasty treats. Dry him off with a
   towel, have him hop out, and praise him
   mightily. Continue this procedure once every
   two days or so, gradually increasing the time and
   the amount of water you pour on him. After a

few weeks, he should be ready to endure a bath
without much objection. Just remember to
always give him treats and praise and to increase
the water and duration very slowly.

How to Bathe Your Dog

First, purchase a hose attachment for the faucet of your tub.
Available in most pet shops, it will allow you to wet down
and rinse off your dog properly. Owners who use a pot or
vessel of some other type to rinse off their dogs rarely get
all of the soap out of the dog's coat, resulting in dried soapy
residue, which can cause a skin rash or a matted coat. Next,
place your dog into the bathtub (or basin, if the dog is a
small one). Attach a lead to his collar, and secure it to one
of the faucets, to prevent him from jumping out of the tub.
If he is a large dog, however, he could break the faucet off
by pulling. In this case, have a friend hold his leash for
you. Now give him a small treat and praise him for being
cooperative. Rinse him down thoroughly with warm (not
hot) water until his entire coat is wet. Breeds with a thick
undercoat (such as the Siberian husky or chowchow) may
take a few extra minutes to wet down, so take your time
and get the water completely worked into the coat, right
down to the skin.

Now, using a veterinarian-approved dog shampoo (not
a human shampoo, designed for our skin, which has a different pH than that of a dog's), apply it to his back, sides,
and underside, then work it in well until a good lather is
created. Be sure to get the lather down all the way to the
skin. Work it down the dog's legs and tail, and then soap
up and lather his chest. Next, apply a small amount of
shampoo to your fingertips and carefully lather the dog's
head and neck areas, making sure not to get any soap into
his eyes.

Thoroughly rinse him off, starting with his head, which
you should tilt upward so as not to let the soapy water drain
into his eyes. Rinse his back and sides well, making sure

to get all the soap out, right to the skin. You may need to turn him around to do a thorough job of it. Then be sure to rinse his belly, legs, and tail.

During the rinsing procedure, lots of fur will probably begin to clog the drain. Be sure to pull the pads of wet fur out of the drain every minute or so to allow proper drainage. You may need to use more than one towel, especially if your dog is a big boy. If he is not frightened by it, consider using a blow dryer as well, to get him as dry as possible. Then take him outside and allow him to shake off. If your dog has a penchant for struggling mightily or biting during a bath, consider letting a professional groomer do it for you. He or she is used to all types of dogs and can easily deal with one who is reticent to endure the ordeal.

If you have a puppy, it is possible to teach him to tolerate or even enjoy the process, if started early on. Be casual and fast, while praising him the entire time. Try to bathe the puppy at least once a month, even if it means just using plain water, to keep him conditioned to the procedure. During the bath, talk happily to him and give him a few small treats. If you're lucky, he will learn to look forward to his monthly cleaning.

BEGGING

DESCRIPTION

When your dog makes a pest out of himself every time you are either preparing food or actually eating, you can be pretty sure he is begging for a handout. He will rub against you, stare at you, jump up at you, and perhaps even paw at you, all in an effort to get you to surrender a morsel of food. Some dogs will try to jump right up onto the counter or dinner table in an effort to score a tasty treat.

WHY YOUR DOG IS DOING THIS

Several factors could be causing your dog to beg incessantly. First, you may be underfeeding her. An underfed dog will out of necessity try to find more to eat and may resort to begging. Most owners feed their dogs enough, however, and can tell if their pets are underweight simply by looking and feeling. If you are in doubt, though, consult your veterinarian, who will determine an ideal weight for your dog. Then all you need do is weigh her once a month to determine if she is at her ideal weight. If she is, you know she is begging for other reasons.

If your dog was once a stray or shelter animal, at one time she may have had to struggle to get food. If this is so, she might retain a very high food drive for much of her life, which could precipitate the begging behavior.

The most common cause of begging behavior in a dog, though, comes from the actions of the owner, who may have gotten into the habit of too often giving his or her dog treats and leftovers throughout the day. By doing so, the well-meaning owner conditions his or her dog to beg. In combination with this, owners of begging dogs often have poor control over their pets, who tend to be dominant dogs with enough smarts to learn how to train their owners into giving them tasty tidbits whenever they want them. Unknowingly, the owner who does so loses more and more pack status until he or she is plainly viewed as a subordinate. The dog enjoys a sense of power and gets fat in the process.

SOLUTION

To minimize begging behavior in your dog, try the following:

1. Make sure your dog is at her proper weight, to ensure she is getting enough food.

2. Feed her on a regular schedule instead of free-feeding all day. By doing so you will be able to teach her that she gets to eat at a prescribed time each day, instead of at any time. Her hunger pangs will peak right at feeding time, instead of at random times during the day. Eventually she will realize that food is no longer available any time she wants.

3. Give her treats only when you are trying to encourage a particular behavior. If you feed her random treats throughout the day, you will condition her to beg for more.

4. Never feed your dog from your dinner plate. Also, do not feed her food intended for human consumption, as this tends to teach her that she has equal status with you. Everything you do with your dog should teach her that, though loved, she is below you in the pecking order.

5. Never give your dog food while you are preparing a meal at the kitchen counter. If you choose to give her something, place it in her food dish instead, at her prescribed dinnertime.

If while you are in the kitchen or at the table your dog continues to jump on you in an effort to beg, simply keep a spray bottle filled with water and a teaspoon of vinegar handy. When she jumps up, give her a spritz right in the mouth while saying, "No!" She will quickly get the idea.

CAR SICKNESS

DESCRIPTION

Some dogs, especially puppies or dogs less than a year old, will get sick while riding in a car. Your carsick dog may vocalize quite a bit and may also vomit, pant heavily, or drool. On subsequent trips, she may show a real aversion to getting into the car or travel crate, as she readily remembers her last experience as being nearly unbearable.

WHY YOUR DOG IS DOING THIS

Some dogs, like persons, are simply more sensitive to the unpredictable movements of a car than are others. The lateral, vertical, and rotational motions, combined with the constant accelerations and decelerations, cause such dogs' balance centers in their inner ears to go awry, bringing on the nausea and dizziness.

Outdoor dogs who rarely leave their yards or pens, as well as geriatric pets who sleep most of the day and rarely accompany their owners in the car, are very apt to get carsick, often when being taken to the veterinarian, groomer, or boarding facility. Dogs who are exposed to riding in cars from early on become accustomed to the event very quickly and rarely suffer any symptoms. It is just a matter of getting used to the unique motions of the car.

SOLUTION

Whether your carsick dog is four months old or ten years old, the two keys to getting her to enjoy car rides are:

1. Convincing her that car rides are fun.
2. Slowly acclimating her to the motions of a car.

If your dog has gotten sick in the car before, odds are she won't treasure getting into the vehicle again. That therefore becomes your first task. You have to teach her that the car is a desirable place to be. The best way to start doing that is feeding her in the car while it is parked, with the engine off. Wait for dinnertime, when she is good and hungry, then bring her and her food bowl out to the car. Open the back door (or hatchback), place the food down, and encourage her to jump in and chow down. Praise her lavishly as she eats. For the first few times keep the door open, but hold onto her leash. After that, close the hatch or door, then get into the car yourself, sitting in the driver's seat. After she has finished, praise her, then bring her back into the home.

After a week of feeding her in this manner, continue to do so, except start the engine when she is about halfway through with her food. If she stops eating, just sit there calmly; do not comfort her at all, as this would be rewarding her for being worried. Just sit there; she will eventually go back to her meal. Repeat this for at least three or four days before moving on.

Next, begin taking her out to the car several times each day, putting her in, starting the engine, and giving her treats and praise. You should do so at least four or five times a day for about a week. At this point you can stop feeding her full meals in the car. Let each session last for at least ten minutes.

Next, put her in the car, toss a treat into the back, then put the car in gear and drive, very slowly, up and down the driveway or in the street in front of your home. Try to drive as smoothly as possible, with no sudden braking and no turning. Do this several times a day for at least three days before moving on. From this point on, schedule the sessions at times when she has as little food in her belly as possible, to minimize the chances of her vomiting.

Gradually increase the distance you travel, and throw in a few turns as well. Always remember to praise her, but consider eliminating the treats at this point. Within two or three days, you should be able to slowly drive around the neighborhood without her getting ill. After two weeks of this, try taking her for a longer drive, perhaps using the freeway. Visit a friend within ten or fifteen minutes of your home. Once there, praise your dog mightily for not getting ill.

From this point, it is recommended that you keep your dog in a travel crate while in the car. In addition to protecting her and you in the event of an accident, the crate will serve to keep her still and to prevent her from watching the road and the sights go by at a fast pace, a factor that can often increase the chances of her becoming ill.

If you live in a busy urban environment and rarely drive, your dog may never get the opportunity to ride in a car and so might be more prone to car sickness. To avoid this, try to take your city dog for a ride every now and then, even if it's on a local bus (if it allows dogs) or in a taxi or a friend's car.

As you can see, the solution to canine car sickness is simply a very gradual, lengthy acclimatization to the experience of riding in a car. If this is done in slow, deliberate steps, your dog should eventually learn to enjoy her rides in the car, Just make sure that she goes for at least two or three rides each week, to keep her "immunity" up.

CHASING

DESCRIPTION

Some dogs just love to chase anything that happens to be moving by, be it a car, motorcycle, jogger, playing child, or bicycle. If one of these moving objects passes by such dogs, they immediately give chase, barking and perhaps nipping along the way. Dogs with a propensity to chase will even try to do so when on-leash, during walks with their owners. These dogs sometimes send owners flying down the street or else break free and take off. Many dogs with an aptitude to chase end up getting either lost, or else struck and killed by cars.

WHY YOUR DOG IS DOING THIS

Several reasons can explain why your dog has a desire to chase things. A number of instinctive drives can play a big part in it, particularly if your dog is a herding breed or one with a high territorial drive. Dogs with a high prey drive (such as sight hounds, Siberian huskies, and most terriers) can also exhibit a desire to chase other dogs, as well as nearly any other animal that put in an appearance.

A spoiled, undisciplined dog is also highly likely to chase something or someone if the mood suits. Owners with little or no control over their dogs tend to relinquish the leadership spot, leading to canines who do pretty much as they please, including running away, chasing other animals or people, and disappearing. Likewise, dogs with no rules to follow don't really know any better and will simply take off after a car, jogger, bicycle, or animal because that is what their instincts tell them to do.

In addition, owners who play chase games with their dogs unknowingly reinforce and encourage their pets to do so with other individuals, much to their dismay. Fido has a hard time telling the difference between chasing you around the backyard and chasing a jogger down the block.

SOLUTION

The first and best way to prevent your dog from chasing people or cars down the street is to make sure he cannot run around loose on your property. No dog, especially one without rules, should be left loose and unsupervised, for the dog's own safety as well as the safety of others. If you had decent control, your dog wouldn't be terrorizing the neighborhood. Any dog who has shown a desire to chase should be contained or else on the end of a leash. Doing so may save your dog's life and help you avoid a costly lawsuit.

Train your dog to obey certain basic commands, including *sit, down, stay, come,* and *don't pull* (when on-leash). Make sure to attend an obedience class at a local Humane Society or at a private training facility in your area; doing so will aid you in gain leadership and control over your dog. Well-trained dogs will stop in their tracks and come whenever commanded to do so. Poorly trained dogs will ignore their owners completely (except at dinnertime).

If your dog has a tendency to chase cars, you can try this exercise. Clip his leash onto his training collar, and then take him out to the edge of the road, preferably one where he has done some chasing before. Allow him to stand facing the road while you linger behind him, holding the leash with two hands. Be sure to have some slack in the leash. Now just wait until a car comes down the road. As soon as one does, get ready and watch your dog. The moment he shows any sign of pulling or chasing, jerk hard on the leash twice, toward yourself, while simultaneously saying, "No!" in a commanding voice. The correction should be firm enough to break his concentration on the car. Too soft a correction will only serve to increase his desire to chase, so be sure to give the leash two good jerks with both hands, snapping it straight toward your thighs. Afterward, walk the dog up and down the street a few yards, then position yourself and the dog again, in hopes that another car will come. Repeat the corrections if necessary. When you see the dog begin to think twice before attempting to lunge after the car, praise him and give him a treat. Work this at least once or twice each day until he really gets the idea. You can also require him to sit or lie down as well, as a way to further occupy his mind.

The next exercise to try after working with the leash begins by attaching a fifteen- or twenty-foot lead to his training collar and then setting him up the same way you did with the shorter leash. With him by the side of the road, walk away from him until he is at least ten or twelve feet from you. Then simply work the exercise the same way, correcting him firmly for attempting to chase a car (or anything else that happens by). By moving yourself farther away from him, you help lessen your direct influence and allow the dog to begin thinking independently, without you on his mind, the way you would be when right beside him. Work this until he shows no signs of chasing behavior.

Next, be sure to never play chase games with your dog. If you do now, stop and instruct all family members (especially kids) to do the same. Instead, teach your dog to come to you reliably. Doing so will still allow him to run and have fun; it just won't encourage the chasing behavior. To work the *come* (or *recall*) command, go into a quiet backyard and attach the long lead to your dog's collar. Allow him to amble about while you slowly increase the distance between the two of you. Then crouch down and in an exciting, animated, happy voice, say *"Fido, come here!"* Clap your hands, slap your thigh, and make lots of commotion. Also, have a dog treat out in one hand. Odds are he will come to you readily. When he does, give him the treat and praise him. If he ignores you, give him a light jerk while saying, "No!", then call him happily again. Remember that at no time should he ever not come to you when called; if need be, actually pull him in toward you. When you command your dog to do something, you cannot ever let him succeed at ignoring or disobeying, as doing so will teach him that you aren't to be taken seriously.

If you are about to purchase a new dog and have lots of children, cars, bicycles, and pedestrian traffic close to your home, consider avoiding the herding breeds as well as terriers or any breed with a high territorial or prey drive, as these dogs will tend to instinctively chase and "protect." Though any dog can be taught not to do so, it might be better to go with a more gregarious breed such as a golden retriever, Newfoundland, beagle, poodle, or keeshond, as these have much less of an inclination to chase.

CHEWING

DESCRIPTION

Normally a habit of puppies in the teething stage, chewing on an appropriate, veterinarian-approved chew toy is an acceptable habit that needs to be performed until the dog's permanent teeth come in. Unfortunately, puppies will often chew on anything handy, including valuable items in the home and electrical wiring. The puppy will find something with just the right texture and chew on it avidly. Some adult dogs never quite outgrow the chewing habit and continue to chew, to the chagrin of the owners, who often have to replace destroyed items in the home.

WHY YOUR DOG IS DOING THIS

Teething puppies need to chew to relieve the discomfort of teething and to help the erupting adult teeth come through the gums. If no specific chew toys are provided for them, they will select some item in the home to gnaw on. Often this can be wiring, shoes, clothing, or even furniture. In the case of wiring, this habit could cause the death of the pet. Adult dogs rarely present owners with a chewing problem unless they have for some reason not outgrown the behavior or have some ongoing dental or gum problem whose pain is relieved by chewing. Though adult dogs love to chew on objects such as bones, rawhide, or hard plastic or rubber toys, most will limit their chewing to these selected items and not things you consider valuable. A few adults might never break out of the puppy chewing phase, however, especially if the behavior is unintentionally reinforced by owners. Owners who never remove valuable items from a puppy's environment or who do not discipline a dog for destroying a good pair of leather shoes can end up with an adult dog who continues this expensive habit.

SOLUTION

All puppies should be provided with a few safe chew toys during the day to satisfy the need to chew. The toys should be made of a hard rubber or plastic material and not rawhide, as rawhide closely resembles finished leather in texture. If you tell your puppy that it's OK to chew on rawhide, you are also telling her that leather is allowable. Plus, chunks of rawhide increase in size once in the puppy's stomach and have been known to cause life-threatening intestinal blockages.

Your local pet shop will have a variety of safe toys for your puppy to chew on. Avoid toys with buttons, stringy materials, or pieces that can break off and choke the pet. If you feel that your puppy must have a natural animal substance to gnaw on, consider purchasing a few cow or pig hooves, also available at the local pet shop. Made of cartilage, hooves do not have a leathery texture and do not swell once inside the stomach. Take care to remove a hoof from your puppy or dog once it gets whittled down to a size that could be swallowed, as this could cause choking.

To get your puppy interested in chewing on a rubber or plastic toy, introduce it by teasing the puppy with it to invoke her prey drive instincts. Scoot the toy around on the floor back and forth in front of her; tease her with it until she wants it badly, then let her have it. You might even consider spreading a small amount of meat-flavored baby food on a portion of the toy to really get the puppy excited. Then just let her chew on it to her heart's content.

At the same time, you need to discourage your puppy from chewing on items that either have value to you or might hurt her. Make sure to hide all wires under the carpeting or else tape them down securely with duct tape. With wires such as the telephone cord, which needs to be out in the open, try spraying it down every so often with a repellent such as Bitter Apple spray. You can also try wiping them down with a soap-and-water mixture, which will taste very bitter to the dog. If the problem is severe, try applying hot mustard or hot sauce to exposed wires or any other chewed-on item. The pet should get the message.

Adult dogs who have never lost the chewing desire should be treated in the same manner. Also, be sure to pick up and store away any item you do not want your dog to chew up. Put away shoes, belts, gloves, television and VCR remote controls, dirty laundry, and anything your dog likes to chew on. In their place, leave acceptable chew toys.

In addition, when you catch your dog or puppy in the act of chewing on a forbidden item give her a quick spray with water from a water pistol or plant sprayer bottle while simultaneously saying, *"No!"* To make it more effective, mix a teaspoon or two of white vinegar into the water bottle. Never hit the dog or throw anything at her.

CHILDREN, INTOLERANCE OF

DESCRIPTION

Most dogs love to play and romp with children. Some, however, cannot deal well with a child's antics and, if unable to find a quiet spot away from the action, might resort to growling or nipping. Or an incident might occur while the dog is eating as a playful toddler carelessly puts his or her hands into the dog's food bowl. Older dogs, generally less tolerant of children than younger ones, might growl or nip at a child for trying to wrestle or for attempting to take away their favorite toys. Whatever the cause, a dog who develops an intolerance for children (especially those under ten years of age) will tend to shy away from them, preferring instead to find a quiet section of the home to escape to. When forced to interact with children, intolerant dogs may growl or bare their teeth first, as a warning to stay away. If this message is not heeded, nipping or serious biting can occur. This unfortunate occurrence often leads to the destruction of the offending animal.

WHY YOUR DOG IS DOING THIS

Though children and dogs normally get along famously, often there can develop situations that cause the dog in question to react aggressively toward a child. First, breed can have an effect on relations between dogs and children. Reserved breeds such as the chowchow, shar-pei, saluki, Afghan, Lhasa apso, and Pekingese tend to have problems relating to children, particularly those who roughhouse, pinch, poke, or pull on hair. Toy breeds such as the Chihuahua, miniature pinscher, Italian greyhound, and Pomeranian might also become extremely intolerant of children, as being so tiny makes a dog much more concerned about getting injured.

The dog's basic temperament can also play a large factor; fearful, timid dogs will shy away from boisterous children in order to feel safe. Extremely dominant dogs might also quickly tire of a very physical child's actions, as these can appear to be challenges to the dog's perceived status. The dominant dog might also nip or bite a child over a possession issue; a toy or piece of clothing that the dog covets, when taken by the child, could incite an aggressive response from the pet.

Most dogs covet their food. Though yours should allow you to pick up his food bowl whenever necessary, he might not recognize the same level of authority in a three-year-old child who attempts to move the dog's bowl or play with the food inside. A small child simply will not be perceived as a dominant pack member by most dogs; because of this, your dog may feel he has the right to discipline the toddler for interfering with dinnertime.

Some dogs will become intolerant of a child who attempts to take away an object the dog covets, such as a toy or blanket. Every member of the "pack" deserves to have control over some items; if one member attempts to usurp this, aggression can result. So, if a child continually tries to steal a dog's possession, bad behavior can happen. Some overly dominant dogs, however, will assume that everything under the sun belongs to them, including children's toys and whatever else happens to be on the floor at the time. This type of dominant pet has no respect for the other "pack" members and attempts to guard any and all objects. When the child in question tries to get his or her toy back, trouble occurs.

By far the biggest cause of a dog becoming intolerant of children is uninvited roughhousing on the part of the children. Playing is one thing; jumping all over dogs and pulling on their ears, fur, and tails is another. Just a few episodes like this can sour a dog on children forever.

SOLUTION

A number of steps can be taken to lessen your dog's intolerance of children. They include the following:

- ◆ Teach your children to respect your dog's dinnertime. Tell them not to play with the dog or his food while he is eating.
- ◆ Teach your children not to take your dog's possessions away from him, especially items such as a chew toy or a favorite tennis ball.
- ◆ Make it clear to your children that undue roughhousing is a real no-no, especially with a small dog, an old one, or a reserved or timid animal.

◆ Eliminate chase and keep-away games between your dog and your children, which only serve to increase possessive instincts and also show the dog how physically superior he is to them. This creates a dominant mind-set for the dog, which can lead to trouble. Instead, have them play fetch with the dog, or have the children work the *recall* or *come* command, using treats as a reward. The dog can come to one child, then another, then another, in a "round-robin" fashion, each time being rewarded with a treat. This is fun for all and also teaches the dog to obey the children.

◆ Instruct your children never to startle your dog while he is sleeping, as it could lead to a biting incident.

◆ Supervise the children and the dog whenever they are interacting, and discipline either when some incorrect behavior is exhibited.

◆ Show your children how to correctly and gently pet your dog, and instruct them never to pull on his fur, ears, or tail.

◆ Discipline your dog whenever he steals a child's possessions or when he growls or nips at a child without good reason. The discipline should come in the form of a leash correction followed by isolation, preferably in a travel crate in a darkened room, away from all family members, for an hour or so. If your dog is extremely dominant (especially with your children), consider keeping a six-foot leash on him while in the home to allow you to correct him whenever necessary. Never hit the dog, however, as this can escalate the problem.

◆ Teach the dog that a new baby is a wonderful thing and not a competitor. Whenever your dog is around your newborn, praise him lavishly and give him treats. Also, consider placing one of the baby's blankets in the dog's crate (or wherever he sleeps) to acclimate him to the scent. Never ignore the dog in favor of the baby, as this can cause the dog to view the child as a usurper and an unwanted competitor. In the dog's mind, the baby should mean more, not less, attention.

COPROPHAGY, OR STOOL-EATING

DESCRIPTION

Coprophagy can occur in dogs who are exposed to the feces of various species, particularly cats. The dog in question, much to the owner's dismay, will simply consume small quantities of stool at various times, with no predictable frequency. Most often a dog will raid a cat's litter box or find cat stool outside on your property, deposited there by a local cat. This habit, in addition to being highly disgusting, can often lead to a viral, bacterial, or parasitic infestation in your dog.

WHY YOUR DOG IS DOING THIS

Though it is often hard to completely understand why a dog might choose to consume feces, several explanations come to mind. First, the feces of some animals may actually give off an appetizing aroma to some dogs, due perhaps to additives that may have been in the food eaten by the originator of the stool in question. Cat stool has a particularly strong attraction for many dogs, perhaps due to the high meat content of the feline diet. Or your stool-eating dog might be suffering from a dietary deficiency of some type and somehow trying to supplement his diet to alleviate the problem. A dog who once spent time as a stray might also have developed the habit, as feces do contain very small amounts of nutrients and might have been at times all that the animal could find to eat.

SOLUTION

If your dog spends time out in the backyard and is eating the stool of other animals deposited there, there is little you can do to stop the behavior, as most of the time you won't be present when the act occurs. You could try to modify the behavior by lacing some stool with hot sauce, then leaving it in an easily found spot in the yard. Doing so several times just might cure your dog of this disgusting habit. The only sure way to stop your dog from eating feces when you are not around is keeping him indoors.

If keeping your dog indoors while you are gone is not an option for you, the next step is to determine if your pet is suffering from a dietary deficiency, causing him to eat feces in an attempt to correct the problem. To do this, you will need to have your veterinarian run some tests to determine if your dog is low in some essential nutrient such as protein, fiber, or some necessary vitamin or mineral that he senses might be contained in the stool.

You should also attempt to keep your property as free from animal stool as possible by going out there at least once or twice par day and disposing of any feces you can find. If you suspect your neighbor's cat is using your yard as a bathroom, have a talk with your neighbor in an attempt to keep the pet off your property. As a last option, put in a call to the local animal control facility to register a complaint.

If you have a cat, take care to locate her litter box in a place that your dog cannot get to. Either place it in a room with a door that is tethered to open only a few inches or else locate it high up enough off the floor to prevent the dog's access. Keep your cat's litter box well scooped, to minimize its odor, something your dog will home in on.

CRATE, AVERSION TO

DESCRIPTION

Many dog owners opt to utilize travel crates for a variety of reasons, be it for transporting their dogs in cars, housebreaking or disciplining or to give their dogs quiet, warm, cozy places to sleep or get away from noisy, chaotic activity. Unfortunately, some dogs quickly learn to dislike or even fear travel crates and will actively resist going into one or else bark, whine, and yelp for hours if forced to stay in one for a period of time. A dog who hates being crated may also attempt to break out by chewing, gnawing, or ramming the door or sides. If this occurs, the crate can become damaged, as can the dog's teeth, paws, and nails.

WHY YOUR DOG IS DOING THIS

The most common cause of a dog fearing a crate is the owner improperly introducing his or her dog to it. Be he a puppy or adult dog, forcing your dog into a crate for the first time and then leaving him all alone is a sure way to get him to hate the thing and to try like heck to avoid going in it again.

Many puppies develop a dislike for the crate because they are often forced to spend time in them right after being separated from their litters and mothers. The separation anxiety eight-week-old puppies feel become connected, in their doggie minds, to the crate.

Adult dogs who have never spent a day in a crate will not enjoy the experience, especially if their owners failed to slowly acclimate the pets to it. Such dogs may panic and actually hurt themselves in an attempt to get out. Remember that dogs become very used to routine; ask a six- or eight-year-old dog who has never experienced confinement to suddenly tolerate hours in a small box, and you are asking for trouble.

Some dogs develop a dislike for the crate as a result of having experienced car sickness on a regular basis. Many owners transport their dogs in crates; if your dog becomes physically ill or frightened in a car, these can both easily become associated, in the dog's mind, with the crate itself. The dog thinks; *Every time I am in this box I get sick.* No wonder he hates the thing.

If your dog has at some time-eliminated while in a crate and was then forced to stay in the crate for hours before being let out, he might have developed a strong dislike for going in the crate again. Though likely to occur only if the dog is ill, this can also occur with a puppy who is in the process of being housebroken.

SOLUTION

First, understand that the use of a travel crate is in no way cruel to your dog. Dogs are denning animals by nature; in the wild, they seek out small, close spaces such as burrows or tight caves in order to keep warm, sleep safely, and give birth to and raise young. Using a crate to housebreak your puppy is also a normal, effective technique, one that takes advantage of the dog's instinctive desire to keep his sleeping area clean. By providing your puppy or adult dog with a crate you actually give him a place he can call his own, one that is warm, safe, snug, and quiet. Most dogs grow to love their crates, using them without ever being asked to. When your dog wants to nap or get away from lots of activity, he can simply crawl into his nice, cozy crate and take a siesta.

Whether your dog is a puppy or an adult dog, he must be properly acclimated to a crate. You cannot simply toss him in, lock the door, and leave. Here are the steps you should take to get a dog to feel comfortable being in a crate:

1. First, purchase a crate that is properly sized for the dog in question. If you want to use the crate to housebreak your dog (be he a puppy or an adult), be sure to use one that is only large enough to allow the pet to lie down, stretch out, and stand up. It should not be large enough for him to easily move from the front to the back, as this will permit the pet to move to the rear of the crate, eliminate, then move to the front of the crate. The idea behind using a crate to housebreak is to take advantage of the dog's instinctive dislike for eliminating where he sleeps. Using a smaller crate will ensure a clean environment and also help delay the dog's desire to eliminate. If your dog is a puppy of a larger breed, you will have to purchase more than one crate in his lifetime, as he will quickly outgrow the first one. Consider using a plastic or fiberglass crate; the wire cages, due to their open designs, tend not to give the dog any sense of security and will also not contain any waste materials that the dog might accidentally produce while in it.
2. Next, begin making your dog feel as if the crate is the best thing in the world. How? By feeding him in it. At first, take the door off its hinges and simply place the dog's food bowl inside the crate, near its opening. If the pet is hungry, he will stick his head in and eat. Over the course of two days, move the food bowl farther and farther back until it is finally all the way inside the crate. At this point, replace the crate door.

Then, while the dog is busy eating, quietly close the door and latch it. Make sure to stay close by. When the dog is done eating, open the door and let him out, praising him lavishly.

3. Over the next few days, continue to feed him in the crate, with the door closed. This time, however, leave him in the crate for a few minutes after he has finished while you sit on the floor nearby. Gradually increase the time he stays in the crate after dinner until he can tolerate it for an hour with no problem (after which you should take the dog out to eliminate). This is the basic technique used to housebreak a dog with a crate.

4. From this stage you should stop feeding your dog in the crate and simply use a few treats tossed into it to encourage him in. You do not want to have a dog with a full belly spending an entire night in a crate, as this would almost ensure that he would have an accident. Try this at night, when it is time for all of you to go to sleep. Locate the crate next to your bed, so that the dog feels comfortable, secure, and protected. Consider placing a chew toy into the crate, as well as a soft blanket or even a small piece of your own clothing, which will have your scent on it, a comforting distraction for the dog. After the dog goes in, close the door of the crate, then get into bed and read a book while your dog settles down. If you have followed the previous instructions, he shouldn't be upset or panicked at this point. If he is somewhat vocal, try to ignore him. If you respond to whimpering or barking, he will learn that his vocalizations will cause you to let him out or at least respond. Just ignore him unless it becomes too loud. In this case, simply rap on the top of the crate with

your knuckles and say, *"No! Quiet!"*

5. After a day or two of this, begin crating your dog for short periods of time while you are home but not necessarily in the room with him. Go in and out and go about your business. Just make sure that you enter and exit the room at least every five minutes or so to let your dog know you are still there. Consider keeping a radio on in the room, tuned to a talk radio station. This will act to soothe the dog and to also drown out any sounds of you moving about. You want your dog to settle down instead of fixate on your activity, so that you can eventually leave the home for periods of time and not have him focus on that thought.

6. Gradually increase the amount of time in between your visits to the dog until you are able to be gone for at least half an hour to an hour. Each time you come back, make less and less direct contact with the dog. Simply go into the room for a moment to retrieve an item, then leave, without saying anything to the dog. This will make your coming and going less of an event to get excited over.

7. Finally, begin closing the door to the bedroom and quietly leaving the home for a few minutes. Listen quietly to hear if he is settled or not. Be sure to leave the radio on a bit louder, to cover the sound of your opening and closing the door to your home as you exit and then reenter. Gradually extend the time you are gone until the dog can comfortably be in the crate for several hours while you are gone.

It is important not to leave your young puppy alone in a crate for long periods of time the first few days you have him home. Let him sleep in the crate next to your bed, but wait at least two weeks before you decide to let him stay all by himself for more than half an hour. Remember that he has just been separated from his mother and siblings and is probably feeling a good bit of separation anxiety.

Be sure to follow the advice given in the section titled "Car Sickness" before attempting to transport your dog by car in a travel crate. By doing so, you will ensure that your dog will not become sick in the crate, an event that could lead to an aversion to being inside one.

If your dog ever does accidentally eliminate in his crate, be sure to clean it out thoroughly before using it again. Use soap and water, plus a small amount of bleach, to kill any germs present. If the dog had a blanket in with him, be sure to wash it well and to also spray it down with an odor neutralizer product, available at any pet store. Doing so will remove any trace of the scent of his feces or urine, which, if left, might encourage him to eliminate in the crate again.

Once your dog is effectively housebroken, it should no longer be necessary to keep him in a crate while you are gone (except if he is being destructive when alone). Continue to leave the crate available to him, however, as he will see it as his own little sanctuary and will go there to rest.

CROTCH SNIFFING

DESCRIPTION

This annoying canine habit is evidenced by dogs rudely sticking their snouts into places where they, quite frankly, do not belong. The behavior will often occur to guests with whose scent your dog is not familiar. This is the same way your dog would greet an unknown dog outside his pack.

WHY YOUR DOG IS DOING THIS

To your dog, a human guest is an outsider, who must be investigated. As the hind quarters are the standard place a dog sniffs a pack outsider, sniffing guests' crotches can be seen as an instinctive reaction on the dog's part (however obnoxious it might seem). Just watch two dogs at the park greet each other; invariably they sniff at each other's back areas even before facing each other.

In addition, humans present a wide array of smells to a dog, whose nose is hundreds of times more sensitive than our own. Laundry detergents, perfumes, fabric softeners, sweat, deodorants, hygiene products, and moisturizing lotions can all present an irresistible lure to a dog. Also, any woman close to or experiencing menstruation is very likely to attract this type of attention from the family dog.

SOLUTION

Fortunately, this annoying and embarrassing habit can be minimized fairly easily. If you know that your dog is likely to sniff at a guest's private areas, clip her leash on well in advance of the guest coming over to your home. Then, while holding the leash, go to the door with the dog and let the guest in. If at any time the dog attempts to perform her obnoxious behavior, give her a quick jerk on the leash while simultaneously saying, "No!" in a firm, commanding voice. Then bring the dog into the living room and have her lie down. If she doesn't have this level of obedience yet, simply hold onto her leash. Let your guest sit in a chair next to a table with a plant sprayer bottle filled with water (and a teaspoon or so of white vinegar) sitting on it. Have the guest hold the sprayer; then release your dog from the down position or just let go of the leash. If she immediately tries to sniff at your guest's crotch, he or she should spray the dog right in the nose while saying, "No!" in a commanding tone. After one or two sprays, your dog should get the message. Then give the guest a dog treat or two and have him or her call the dog over. The guest should ask your dog to sit, then give her the treat and some physical praise. The reason for this is to let the dog know that appropriate contact is welcome; only the inappropriate sniffing is not.

DEPRESSION

DESCRIPTION

Dogs suffering from depression will often show a marked reduction in activity and may not be as gregarious as they once were. Appetite may decline and elimination habits may also suffer. In addition, the depressed dog may vocalize and sleep more than a well-adjusted animal and be more irritable than normal.

Recognizing depression in a dog can be quite difficult, as its symptoms can closely mirror those of any number of physical ailments. Only after a visit to the veterinarian has ruled out any physical abnormalities can the diagnosis of depression be verified.

WHY YOUR DOG IS DOING THIS

The list of causes for canine depression is as long as that for humans. Almost anything could cause your dog to fall into a depressive funk. It really depends on the dog. Several factors, however, are often to blame for a dog falling into a prolonged depression. These include:

Loss of another pet or person in the household. Because your dog is a pack animal and can become as emotionally attached to another pet or person as yourself, the sudden removal of that individual from her life can be a traumatic and depressing experience, and one that can take a long time for the dog to get over.

Change of environment. Moving to another home can worry and depress a dog, who becomes very attached to a "territory" and stressed at its sudden loss. The longer your dog has been at one home, the more likely she will become depressed over leaving it.

Change in food. Often something as seemingly trivial (to us) as a dietary change can throw a dog for an emotional loop.

Change within the environment. Changes in home décor (such as new furniture or carpets) can set sensitive dogs off and cause them to lament. Suddenly kicking your dog out of your bed or bedroom at night can hurt her feelings. Even the disappearance of a favorite toy can often depress a dog for a period of time. The addition of any strange new sights, sounds, or scents might also upset your sweet pooch for a time.

Change of schedule. Doing things differently or at a different time can alter a dog's mood. For instance, if you change to a night shift at your job and are suddenly gone all night long, your dog could become stressed and sullen. Feeding your dog at a different time of day or even having a regular visitor suddenly stop showing up can upset some dogs.

Boredom. Dogs who have very little stimuli in their world can become depressed and lethargic. Reducing or removing a familiar, pleasing activity in your dog's life (such as midday walk) might also depress her.

Lack of exercise. As is the case with boredom, any dog who gets little or no exercise each day might eventually become moody and depressed.

Old age. Like people, dogs get depressed over not being

able to do things that were child's play a few years before. The dog who can no longer easily jump into the back of a pickup truck will lament it, just as we might lament not being able to play tennis or golf as effectively as we once did. With dogs, however, old age comes on more suddenly, over a period of just a few years, making it more traumatic for them than it is for us. At least we have twenty or thirty years to get used to the idea.

SOLUTION

The very first step in trying to end your dog's depression is taking her to your veterinarian, who will examine her thoroughly to determine if, in fact, an injury or physical disorder is causing the problem. Remember that dogs, like cats, tend to be stoic about pain and illness; the only sign could closely resemble depression.

If physical discomfort has been ruled out, the next step is to think carefully about your dog's environment. Has it changed at all in the last few weeks? Did you move? Did another pet or person leave or pass away? Did someone new move in? Was there a change of food? Think about anything that might have changed in her life, even if it was something as seemingly trivial as a stinky old toy being thrown away.

Once you come up with a list of changes, attempt to reverse as many of them as possible. Pull that toy out of the garbage, stitch it up, wash it, and return it to your pooch. Switch back to that old food if possible, unless the change was necessary for health reasons. Whatever is fixable fix. Move the food bowl or crate back to where it was. Put the same old talk show back on the radio while you are away. Do whatever you can think of to try to return the status quo.

If you think the loss of another pet might be the cause, think twice before replacing the animal right away. Though the loss might, in fact, be causing your dog's depression, getting a new pet (be it dog or cat) might backfire and cause your old dog to feel threatened or ignored. It's best to wait a while before replacing a lost pet to see if your current dog learns to adjust to the new situation. Instead, consider adding some new toys to her world or taking her for a few extra walks each day. If the depression is being caused by the departure of a person from the home, see if you can arrange for him or her to visit your dog every so often to help assuage her feelings of loss.

If you have changed the dog's schedule somehow, attempt to return to the old way, if possible. If you are now working a different schedule, see if a person your dog knows well can come over for a few minutes while you are gone to keep her company, Often this is enough to pull a sullen dog out of the doldrums.

If your dog is depressed due to boredom, try adding some fun to her life. Get her new toys. Hide treats around the home for her to discover. Teach her some new tricks, or enroll her in an agility class. Play a pet video on the television. Leave an ice cube or a whole egg, still in its shell, in her dish. Whatever you can come up with that interests her will do.

Last, get your dog moving around more. This applies particularly to aging dogs, who get less exercise and stimuli than younger dogs. Play with her, to get her heart pumping. Buy a tennis ball and take her to the park twice a week. Move her food dish to the top of a flight of stairs to get her nose "turned on." Whatever you can do to get her moving around will help perk up her mood.

Most of all, before making major changes in your home or lifestyle, consider how they will affect your dog. If you can't avoid changing something, try to make the transition as gradual as possible, to acclimate her to the new situation.

Some owners of depressed dogs have helped moderate their pets' depression through the use of veterinarian-approved prescription drugs. Numerous mood-altering medications exist that can have the same antidepressant effects on dogs as Prozac and tricyclic drugs have on humans. If your dog's depression hasn't responded to any environmental changes you have made, consider discussing this option with your veterinarian.

DESTRUCTIVE BEHAVIOR

DESCRIPTION

Dogs have the potential of causing major destruction of property in and around the home. This behavior is more likely exhibited by puppies and adolescent dogs than by older pets, and typical results of destructive behavior are torn-up shoes, damaged furniture, ripped carpeting, chewed-up personal belongings, destroyed remote controls, overturned bookshelves, counters in disarray, clothing dragged or deposited in random places, gardens or lawns dug up and destroyed, and overturned houseplants.

WHY YOUR DOG IS DOING THIS

Several factors might be responsible for your dog causing random damage to your home and/or property. First, an unneutered dog (particularly a male) might feel the need to get out of the home and mate but cannot, at least when kept indoors during the day. So, in response to his frustration, the dog may let it out by ripping things up or knocking things over. Or you may simply have a frisky puppy or young dog with lots of energy to burn and plenty of high jinks up his sleeve. In addition, your dog may simply become so bored in a nonstimulating environment that he acts out, destroying things as a means of voicing his frustrations. Timid or worrisome dogs who dread being left alone can also be quite destructive, as can newly adopted dogs who fear abandonment, don't consider your home their territory yet, and may not have any experience being indoors during the day.

Dogs who tend to do lots of damage to the yard might also be acting out frustrations of boredom, containment, or isolation or might simply be prone to digging, as are most dogs (especially terriers). Any dog allowed access to the entire backyard during the day will tend to eliminate in random spots, resulting in the gradual destruction of the grass or gardens.

Whatever the cause, the dog in question has not yet learned what you deem to be proper and improper behavior, probably because you have not taught him what behaviors are acceptable or unacceptable.

SOLUTION

The first step in minimizing destructive behavior in the home is having your dog neutered. Doing so will remove the mating drive and all the nonthinking mayhem that can arise from it.

Next, you must make your home as dog-proof as possible. Do not leave food or dirty dishes on counters or newspapers on the coffee table or chair. Place houseplants in suspended hangers, or secure them in position so the dog can't knock them over. Cover the tops of the pots with round plastic covers (available at department stores and garden supply stores) to prevent your dog from digging into them. Also, pick up after yourself; avoid leaving clothing scattered about, as your dog might decide to drag it around the home for hours or chew it to shreds.

An effective way to minimize destructive behavior in your dog is to create an environment filled with interesting things to do. Place fun toys and chews down on the floor. Buy your dog a travel crate for her to use as an inside doghouse. Leave a few treats down in random places for your dog to find. Move her food dish around. Leave a radio playing softly, tuned in to talk radio. The more you do to make your dog's world more interesting, the less you will have to deal with destructive behavior.

Dogs with lots of pent-up energy need to release it. Otherwise they will wreak havoc in the home when left alone. Sporting breeds such as pointers and retrievers are especially prone to this. To solve the problem, be sure to properly exercise these dogs every day, especially before you plan on leaving the home for a few hours. Taking an energetic dog for a fifteen- or twenty-minute jog once or twice a day can often eliminate destructive behavior and help create a happier, better-adjusted pet. Playing fetch, working the *come* command, or taking the dog for a daily swim can also work to calm the pooch down during the day.

An untrained dog is much more likely to be destructive at home than a well-trained, properly behaved dog. Taking a few obedience classes and reading some books on basic obedience training can help reduce or eliminate destructive behavior, by solidifying in your dog's mind that you are the leader and she the subordinate. Dogs who know the rules rarely destroy the territory of their leader.

Puppies should never be left alone for very long. Doing so invites destruction and can stress the pet out as well. If you must leave your puppy home alone, crate her; don't leave her loose. Doing so will prevent the little one from chewing and ripping things up, as well as help solidify housebreaking habits.

Your newly adopted dog should also be crated when left alone, at least until she gets used to you and her new home. These dogs tend to worry over being abandoned (with good reason). Yours might become extremely worried upon seeing you leave for work for the first time, thinking that she is being abandoned again. A good idea is to schedule the adoption of a new dog with vacation time, so the two of you can have time to bond properly and she can learn to feel safe and secure in her new home. To be safe, crate your newly adopted dog for at least two months while you are gone during the day. Try to have a neighbor or pet sitter come over at least once or twice during the day to let her out and to play with her, as asking a dog to stay in a crate for eight or nine hours is an unreasonable request.

If your dog is destroying your yard, consider moving her into the home instead. That's where she would prefer to be anyway, as it is the den of her pack. Most owners make the mistake of thinking the dog prefers to be outside. That's just not true. All dogs would prefer to be amongst the sounds, sights, and scents of the home. If her housetraining is good, consider bringing her indoors and having a neighbor or pet sitter come over once during the day to let her out.

If having your dog indoors during the day is not an option, consider building a dog run in your yard, instead of allowing her access to the entire property. This will accomplish several things. First, it will save your landscaping. Second, it will tell the dog that the yard is not her territory but yours and that the smaller dog run is hers to do with as she pleases. Reclaiming the yard for your own helps increase your leadership status, which in turn helps reduce bad behaviors. The dog run will also prevent her from eliminating all over the yard, something that prevents owners from using the yard themselves. Your dog will eliminate in a smaller, more confined area, probably in the corner of her new run, ideally a fenced-in area measuring at least six feet by twelve feet. Place a crate or doghouse inside the run to give her a place to rest and keep warm.

Destructive behavior rarely occurs while you are there. If it does, however, feel free to correct your dog dog by spraying her with water from a spray bottle and saying, *"No!"* Do not hit her or throw any objects at her, as this could traumatize the dog and cause more behavior problems.

DIGGING
SEE "DESTRUCTIVE BEHAVIOR."

DRINKING FROM THE TOILET

DESCRIPTION

Many dog owners have heard this annoying yet comical behavior at some time: the sound of prolonged lapping from an extraordinarily large bowl, located nowhere near the dog's normal water bowl. Water drips all over the bathroom floor, and the dog comes sauntering out of the bathroom, obviously very pleased with himself. In rare occurrences, a dog could become ill from this habit, either from ingesting bacteria-laden water or from drinking water treated with a commercially available toilet bowl disinfectant product.

WHY YOUR DOG IS DOING THIS

Because he is thirsty! Seriously, dogs who tend to drink from the toilet often have owners who can be a bit remiss with regard to keeping water in their pets' bowls. Left with no alternative, the dog in question seeks out another source, usually available in the bathroom. In addition to a dearth of water in the dog's bowl, keeping the toilet lid up and the bathroom door open helps encourage the habit. Families with young children often have this problem, as the young ones tend to forget to put the lid down or close the door.

SOLUTION

An easy one. First, make sure fresh water is always available to your dog in his normal water bowl. Next, keep the toilet lid and the bathroom door closed. Finally, instruct all family members to do the same and also not to encourage your dog if he ever does try to drink from the toilet. Just in case, consider not using any of the blue or green toilet cleaning products, as they could sicken your dog in the event he drinks from the bowl.

DROOLING

DESCRIPTION

Some dogs develop a habit of drooling at certain times during the day. Saliva will slowly drip from the pet's mouth and onto the hair below, creating a darkened wet area, more evident in longhaired breeds than in short-. The dog has no way of preventing this, as canine lips don't have the same ability as our own to hold in excess saliva.

WHY YOUR DOG IS DOING THIS

Some breeds are more prone to drooling than others. Saint Bernards, Newfoundlands, mastiffs, Great Danes, rottweilers, and bulldogs all tend to drool, much to the chagrin of their owners.

Dogs suffering from some type of tooth or gum problem may begin to drool, due to the possibility that they cannot close their mouths entirely. A broken tooth, abscess, or oral infection can be quite painful and would easily cause the dog to pant and drool due to stress.

Certain diseases can cause a dog to drool. Rabies, distemper, and other infectious disorders can all have drooling as a side effect, all the more reason for bringing your dog to the veterinarian as soon as possible.

Some dogs learn to drool whenever dinnertime approaches, especially if the smell of food is in the air for long periods of time. This is a natural, "Pavlovian" response of dogs and many other mammals, including ourselves.

Other dogs drool whenever they are being petted, a response to the relaxed, pleasant mood gentle stroking can bring on. Even sleeping dogs can drool on occasion, especially if they are older.

SOLUTION

First, take your drooling dog to the veterinarian, who will examine her thoroughly for signs of gum or tooth disease or a possible abscess in the making. He or she will also attempt to rule out the chance of your dog having any type of infectious disease that could be causing the problem.

If your dog is given a clean bill of health, you can then assume that the drooling is a behavioral response to something in her environment. If the drooling occurs while you are preparing your own dinner, try feeding her just as you begin to cook, instead of during or after. Feeding her in a room other than the kitchen might help also. Consider feeding her two or three times a day instead of once, to minimize her hunger pangs. Also, avoid giving her human food, as this will train her to drool whenever you eat something. Consider having a time during the day when you teach the dog some new behavior and reward her with a treat or two. This will keep her mind active and not so focused on dinnertime and will also help curb her hunger somewhat.

If your dog is of a breed known for drooling, there is not much you can do other than grin and bear it. Some breeders claim that their line of animals drool less, though the possibility of breeding for this characteristic has not been proved as of yet.

If your dog drools in response to petting, there is not much you can do. After all, you do not want to reduce desired physical contact and you wouldn't want to deny her the pleasure of being stroked. Just clean up the excess and be happy that she likes you.

The same goes for a sleeping dog who drools. The fact that your dog is asleep when this happens makes behavioral modification impossible. Just put down some type of absorbent cloth atop her sleeping spot and tell your friends not to laugh.

EATING TOXIC SUBSTANCES AND OBJECTS

DESCRIPTION

A dog who has ingested a toxic substance may quickly go into shock or experience seizures, convulsions, and loss of muscular control, followed by respiratory failure, paralysis, and death. The dog may also have accelerated respiration and heartbeat, dizziness, and dilated pupils. Some less toxic substances may render the dog sleepy or lethargic or irritable and hyperactive. Many toxins will cause a dog to vomit and/or drool, with diarrhea and excess urination also possible.

A dog who has ingested an object (such as an article of clothing, spool of wire, ball, or rock) won't necessarily develop the same rapid, serious symptoms as a dog who has ingested poison but could soon suffer life-threatening complications nonetheless. Apart from the immediate threat of choking, a foreign, indigestible object probably won't be able to pass through the dog's digestive tract, instead getting caught in the stomach or small intestines, where it will irritate, cause infection, and interfere with digestion of food. The dog can eventually die from infection, starvation, internal bleeding, abscess, or a number of other complications. Smaller objects will often pass through dogs but can nonetheless do damage to their digestive tracts.

WHY YOUR DOG IS DOING THIS

Your dog does not know how lethal certain household substances can be. She depends on you to keep them out of her environment. Some toxins (such as antifreeze, certain fertilizers, and cough syrup) may actually taste good to a dog and are therefore readily ingested. If potentially lethal substances are left out in the open, your dog will eventually find them and investigate. Puppies and young dogs are especially prone to poisoning, due to their incredibly curious minds and lack of experience.

Puppies and adult dogs alike often chew on and sometimes swallow foreign objects, for a number of reasons. Most often, a dog will take a particular liking to an article of clothing of yours, due to the scent of it reminding the pet of you. Shoes, socks, undergarments, telephones, remote controls, and T-shirts are particularly susceptible, as these items, contain more of your scent than other objects do. Any item made of leather is also a prime target, as they are considered food by the dog. Whatever the item, many dogs will chew on it for its scent, flavor, or texture. Teething puppies are especially guilty of this, as they need to chew in order to help their adult teeth erupt from the gums.

Many dogs can become obsessed with a favorite object (such as a ball or stuffed toy) and will covet it and chew on it for hours on end. Eventually, this item gets swallowed, either in pieces or whole. A few dogs will even obsess on objects that one wouldn't normally identify as desirable, such as rocks, sticks, paper clips, wire, or rubber bands. Any of these, once swallowed, can cause serious damage or even death.

SOLUTION

The first step in preventing your dog from being poisoned or harmed by ingestion of a dangerous object is knowing what substances can harm her. These include:

- Acetaminophen
- Acid
- Alcohol
- Antifreeze
- Aspirin
- Battery acid
- Chlorine bleach
- Drain cleaner
- Fertilizer
- Gasoline or diesel fuel
- Household cleaners such as Windex, Lysol, and Mr. Clean
- Insecticides
- Motor oil
- Paint
- Prescription drugs
- Solvents
- Rat poison
- Tarnish remover

In addition, many types of house- and garden plants are toxic to dogs. These are covered in the section titled "Plant Eating."

Get all of these substances out of your dog's environment and in securely locked cupboards, preferably located high up in the garage. Remember that dogs are quite curious and adept at getting into tight places, so be sure to take this into account. If your dog has access to the yard, you must be careful about putting fertilizer down on gardens and lawns, as she will spend a good amount of time digging and frolicking all over these areas. Rather than choosing a chemical fertilizer, consider using an organic alternative such as manure, especially for the garden, as it will be safe for the dog to be in contact with. Clean up all oil spills, particularly those on the driveway, in the garage, and on the street, as contact with oil can make your dog ill. Above all, *make sure that no antifreeze is left on the floor, driveway, or street,* as it is highly toxic and can kill your dog if ingested. Antifreeze has a sweet taste that both dogs and cats love, so beware.

Keep all over-the-counter and prescription drugs stored away safely. Some small, agile dogs can actually climb up and open medicine cabinets, so beware. Consider not keeping household cleaners under the kitchen or bathroom sinks, either, as many dogs can easily open these with a flick of a paw.

If your dog has ingested a poisonous substance, you may need to act quickly to save her life. The common treatment is to induce vomiting, unless the poison consumed is of a corrosive nature, such as battery acid, fertilizer, or drain cleaner. Allowing these to come back up will further damage the dog's esophagus and oral cavity. Also avoid inducing vomiting if the dog is having convulsions or is losing consciousness.

To induce vomiting, administer one to three teaspoons of syrup of ipecac, according to the dog's size. For dogs under fifteen pounds, use one teaspoon. For dogs between fifteen and forty pounds use two, and for dogs over forty pounds use three. If this is not available, get as much heavily salted water into your dog as possible. After she has vomited, get her to drink as much water or milk as possible. Force-feed her with a turkey baster if necessary. Then get her to the veterinarian as soon as possible. Also, discuss poisoning with your veterinarian in advance as a precautionary measure.

Be sure to have an emergency telephone number for

your veterinarian at the ready or the listing for a twenty-four-hour clinic. Also, you can call the *National Animal Poison Information Center* at **1-800-548-2423** for expert advice on what to do if your dog has ingested a toxic substance. If all else fails, try 911; someone there may be able to help. Whatever you do, get your dog to a veterinarian as quickly as you can.

Prevention by removal is the only effective way to dissuade your dog from eating toxic substances, as modifying the behavior requires her to actually perform the undesired act at least once or twice and then receive some form of negative reinforcement. It goes without saying that you do not want her to ever perform this undesired act; just one lick at some poisons could be fatal. So it is up to you to prevent this behavior from occurring by removing all toxins from the dog's world.

To prevent your dog from swallowing foreign objects, be sure to dog-proof your home and yard and to keep it that way. This means picking up and removing dirty laundry, children's toys, or any other loose objects from the floor or from wherever the dog is capable of going. Boxes of paper clips or rubber bands, pens and pencils, bottle caps, cardboard boxes, and even spools of wire should be placed out of the dog's reach. At the same time, provide your dog with acceptable chew toys such as a nylon or hard rubber bone, an animal hoof or ear, or a floss or rope toy. If your dog has an obsession with a specific object (say a tennis ball), only allow her access to it when you are there. Otherwise, remove it from her view.

ESCAPING

DESCRIPTION

Some dogs succeed in finding a way out of the home or yard and out into unknown territory, namely, the busy streets or the rural outdoors. The escape is usually made through an open window, gate, or door and less often from an automobile during a time when the dog is being transported. Dogs allowed to wander outside near home sometimes go too far and leave familiar territory, especially those who have not been neutered. Once out of familiar surroundings, a dog can become disoriented and end up being taken in by someone else or captured by an animal control agency.

WHY YOUR DOG IS DOING THIS

Several reasons can explain why your dog might have a desire to escape from his home. First, dogs are curious animals with excellent senses that can sometimes get them into trouble. An open window or door, combined with the scent of a cat or another dog outside, is often all it takes to lure your dog out into what may be a dangerous environment. Leave the front door open for a minute or so, and even the most timid dog is apt to at least investigate.

An unneutered dog (particularly a male) is a prime candidate to make a "break" for it at some time. Upon catching the scent of a female in heat, a male dog can travel as far as several miles from home in an attempt to mate. By the time he finds the female, he may be too far from home to find his way back. Unneutered females can also venture far from home in search of a mate, though they typically won't travel as far.

Dogs whose owners move to new neighborhoods can become homesick for their old territory and might decide to go looking for it. These dogs escape from the new, strange territory and search in vain for the old, becoming lost in the process. Those who escape death from automobiles or other animals often get picked up by animal control agencies, whose shelters rarely keep stray dogs for more than a week or two before euthanizing them.

Newly adopted shelter dogs might try to escape within a few weeks of being adopted in an attempt to find their old owners. It makes no difference how loving the new owners are; if dogs lived for many years with the previous owners, they may try to find their old homes again.

Owners with poor leadership and control over their dogs often do not have the authority to command their dogs to come back to them once off-leash at a park or outside the home. If your dog does not recognize you as his leader he will ignore your pleas to come back and simply go wherever he so desires. In his mind he has the right to do so, as he thinks he is his own boss.

Children often do not have the strength to hold onto a dog's leash while on a walk. This can result in the dog taking off after another animal or just deciding to go for a stroll through the neighborhood. As children rarely have much control over dogs, it becomes nearly impossible for them to call their dogs back.

Dogs who love to dig often escape from fenced-in yards or dog runs. Left by themselves for much of the day, many of these tunneling experts do so out of sheer boredom or out of a desire to go after another animal. Terriers are especially prone to this type of escape, though any dog is capable of it.

SOLUTION

The first step in preventing your dog from escaping and becoming lost is checking all possible escape routes out of the home and yard, making sure that the dog has no way out. Make sure that if a window needs to be opened, a secure screen without tears is in place. The same goes for all doors; if one needs to be open, be sure to have a secure screen door in place, one that doesn't take too long to close on its own. If transporting your dog in the car, do so using a pet carrier, to prevent him from leaping out at an inopportune time. Some dogs do not like car travel and often become stressed by it; give them an out, and they will take it. Prevent this by putting your dog in a secure pet carrier.

If your dog spends time in a yard or dog run, make sure the fence has no openings and that it is high enough to prevent him from jumping out. Also, consider having poured concrete or concrete blocks right up to the edge of the fence, to eliminate the possibility of the dog digging his way to freedom. If this is too expensive a procedure, at least make sure that the fence has no openings along the ground and that you lay down a one-foot-wide strip of chicken wire along the inner perimeter of the fence, which you can cover with a thin layer of dirt and grass or camouflage with ivy. Doing so will quickly dissuade even the most committed digger.

Children are a major cause of dog escapes. They unintentionally leave windows or doors open, allowing the pet a tempting avenue out. They also often cannot hold onto a leash tight enough. If you do have children, talk to them about closing all doors and windows to prevent your pooch from getting outside. Also, teach them how to properly walk the dog and how to wrap the leash around their hands to prevent it from slipping free. If your dog is large and strong, don't expect a child under the age of twelve to be able to take him for a walk.

The best way to dissuade your dog from taking off for parts unknown is having him or her neutered. Doing so will minimize the desire to roam and mate, making it much easier to keep the pet close by. A neutered male won't have the desire to seek out that female in heat a mile away. A neutered female will not have any desire to seek out a mate. Also, neutering will prevent unwanted pregnancies, the biggest cause of dog deaths in the world. If you ever had to witness an entire litter of unwanted puppies being euthanized, you would think twice about allowing your unneutered dog to wander around the neighborhood, breeding indiscriminately.

If you have just recently adopted a dog, be sure to keep a close eye on him for several months and do not allow him to be off-leash until he is properly trained. After a few months, he should consider you his new master, removing the possibility of his searching for his old one.

Owners who fail to establish rules and leadership with their dogs run a much higher risk of their escaping, as these pets think they are their own bosses and will not come when called. Take an obedience class or two and set rules for your dog. Teach him to come when called under different circumstances, including as many distractions as you can come up with. Doing so will ensure that he comes back to you if he suddenly gets loose in a busy area. If you become a fair and consistent leader in your dog's eyes, he will want to come to you, thus preventing the threat of a lost or runaway dog.

Always be sure to place an identification tag on your dog. Attach it to a sturdy collar. Be sure to have your name and telephone number on the tag, along with the dog's name.

One way to prevent your dog from attempting an escape is to make sure he is not bored. Provide him with an interesting environment; supply toys and anything else he finds intellectually appealing. Teach him to perform tricks and work on his obedience skills each day. By doing so you will be diverting much of his energies into his own territory and away from thoughts of escape.

EXCESSIVE PREY DRIVE

DESCRIPTION

Predation on small animals by a domestic dog, though uncommon, can be an upsetting and emotional experience. Some dogs will kill rodents, birds, snakes, or even cats and other dogs, if allowed to roam freely. Dogs with an excessively high prey drive can make the lives of their owners more than a little frightening, and acting on this drive can lead to the euthanization of the pet.

WHY YOUR DOG IS DOING THIS

Dogs are predators and have been for millions of years. Many are very good at stalking and killing other animals. That said, most domestic dogs have been bred to be somewhat more cooperative with other dogs and to be less predatory toward other animals, while still maintaining a strong territorial drive. Your black Labrador retriever may corner a raccoon in the yard but probably won't kill and eat it unless starving.

Some dogs, however, seem to have a much higher prey drive than do others. Terriers, for instance, if given the chance, will happily hunt down and kill rodents. Sight hounds such as the greyhound and Borzoi often cannot be trusted around a rabbit or cat. A male unneutered rottweiler would be much more likely to kill a small stray dog entering his yard than would a golden retriever.

In general, the following breeds have a higher statistical chance of showing excessive prey drive than others:

◆ Akbash
◆ Afghan hound
◆ Borzoi
◆ Greyhound
◆ Ibizan hound
◆ Irish wolfhound
◆ Pharaoh hound
◆ Rhodesian ridgeback
◆ Saluki
◆ Scottish deerhound
◆ Whippet
◆ Most terriers

◆ Rottweiler
◆ Mastiff
◆ Great Dane
◆ Pit bull
◆ Great Pyrenees
◆ Chowchow
◆ Shar-pei
◆ Malamute
◆ Siberian husky
◆ Doberman pinscher
◆ Giant schnauzer
◆ Komondor
◆ Kuvasz
◆ Australian cattle dog
◆ Chesapeake Bay retriever
◆ German shepherd
◆ Bouvier des Flandres

There are of course exceptions; simply owning one of these breeds does not mean that you will have to deal with your dog killing another animal. Your dog's personality, individual temperament, and training will have a big impact on his behavior.

The step from chasing and harassing another animal to actually killing it is, to us, a big one but might not be that much of a leap for the dog, particularly one of the aforementioned breeds, who were bred to hunt, kill, or aggressively defend. When excessive prey drive is exhibited, however, it is less often directed toward other dogs of similar size but rather toward smaller prey animals such as rabbits, rodents, such as squirrels, cats, or birds. In addition, toy breeds such as the Chihuahua, Maltese, and papillon could fall victim to a larger dog with a high prey drive, as these dogs appear more like prey and less like competition to most larger breeds.

Dogs who exhibit a high level of prey drive most often have a genetic predisposition to behave in this way. Some dogs, however, particularly those who have been physically abused or who were separated from their litters at too early an age (before the eighth week), can show profound aggressive tendencies toward other animals, as can dogs who have been trained to attack and kill.

SOLUTION

Owning a dog who has killed another animal can be difficult and stressful, to say the least. Other pet owners deserve to know that their beloved pets will not be harmed or killed by yours. In addition to the heartbreak, legal action taken against you and your dog could result in your pet's destruction and in thousands of dollars in civil penalties levied upon you.

If your dog shows an abnormally high prey drive, you will need to have an experienced canine behaviorist examine him to see how bad the problem is and to help you cope with it. You cannot handle this problem alone; that would be like someone not versed in the use of handguns trying to use one safely and responsibly. Talk to your veterinarian; he or she will surely be able to refer you to a qualified professional behaviorist, who may be able to teach you ways to minimize your dog's predatory tendencies.

Be sure to never allow a dog with an excessively high prey drive to be out and about without close supervision by you. The dog should be either on a leash or safely contained in a home or yard. Do not allow such a dog to run free at a dog park, as this could result in death for another pet. Do not allow this dog to come into close contact with any other pet unless they have grown up together and have a good, loving relationship. Also, do not allow such dogs to interact with small children unless they have developed a loving relationship with one. Even then, do not let the dog alone with a baby or toddler.

By all means, have any highly predatory dog neutered.

Doing so will help minimize aggression and also prevent faulty genes from being passed on to another animal.

Avoid adopting or purchasing any rodents, cats, birds, or other small creatures while owning a dog with a high prey drive. Eventually a bad encounter probably will occur, resulting in a horrific scene. Bringing another dog into the family might also not be a good idea, as the aggressive dog might attack without warning. If the new dog is a small one, death might result.

If, despite all of these precautions, your dog continues to act in a highly predatory manner toward other pets, you may have to consider euthanasia. Though this is an extremely hard decision to make, the safety of others is more important than the continuance of the life of a dangerous animal.

FINICKY EATING

DESCRIPTION

Some dogs seem to barely pick at their food throughout the day, perhaps eating a few bits here and there but never really appearing to chow down. This causes the owners of finicky dogs to leave food out for the entire day, in order to satisfy their discriminating canines. Toy breeds can be especially finicky eaters, as can older dogs.

WHY YOUR DOG IS DOING THIS

Some dogs become spoiled by owners who feed them tasty little tidbits of human food throughout the day. When then presented with a boring dish of dry kibble, most pampered dogs will look up as if to say, *"You're joking, right?"* The end result is a dog who will only eat human leftovers or food with lots of scent to it. Toy breeds, being the most pampered and spoiled, often develop finicky eating habits.

The biggest cause of finicky eating in a dog is the process of *free-feeding*. Many owners who are gone for the day use this method of feeding, which involves leaving dog food out all day and replenishing it whenever the amount appears reduced. This procedure encourages your dog to eat very small amounts of food on an almost continuous basis throughout the day, giving him the appearance of being finicky. The food is always there; why should he become excited at dinnertime?

The appetite of your dog will fall off tremendously if he becomes sick or injured. If you notice that your dog's normally good appetite has taken a nosedive, it may point to sickness or injury.

The appetite of your older dog might fall off substantially during her last few years. A gradually failing body makes digestion and elimination more difficult, causing the pet to eat less in order to avoid discomfort. Tooth decay and gum disease, common in old dogs, can also curb your pet's appetite.

SOLUTION

The best way to feed your dog is to establish definite feeding times during the day and then simply make food available to her for a short window of time, say fifteen minutes or so. Twice a day put the dog's dish down with whatever food you decide to feed her while simultaneously ringing a bell or calling her name. Leave it down for fifteen minutes; if she eats, so be it. If not, pick the food up and store it. Later on in the day, repeat the procedure. If she eats, she eats. If not, remove the food. Eventually she will become hungry enough to get the picture. You may need to repeat this for a day or two; if so, don't worry. Your dog won't let herself starve. Sooner or later she will learn that when the dinner bell rings it's time to get that chow!

Avoid feeding your dog rich human foods throughout the day, as this will spoil her and turn her off her regular food. Limit treats as well, especially with a finicky or obese dog. Also, do not encourage begging!

If your dog normally eats well but has just recently begun shunning food, take her to your veterinarian for a checkup. Sudden changes in appetite can point to illness or injury, so be aware and get her to a professional as soon as you can. You might end up saving her life.

As a dog gets older, you may need to change foods in order to find one more palatable to your aging friend. In addition, consider adding small amounts of fresh meat to his food each day, as an incentive to eat.

Be sure to check your dog's teeth and gums regularly for any abnormalities that could curb the pet's appetite. Broken or chipped teeth, abscesses, and diseased gums can all cause your pooch to avoid food, so be sure to keep her mouth in tiptop shape. Have her teeth cleaned once a year, and brush her teeth at least once a week with a soft toothbrush and some veterinarian-approved doggie toothpaste.

FLATULENCE

DESCRIPTION

No difficulty in describing this uncommon behavior. More of an inconvenience than a misbehavior, flatulence in dogs occurs infrequently. When it does, however, it can be unpleasant and bothersome to owners, who are both embarrassed and inconvenienced by it.

WHY YOUR DOG IS DOING THIS

Often dogs will become flatulent when a certain type of food is fed to them, especially one that isn't one of the dog's staples, such as table scraps or milk products. Foods with too high a percentage of grains or vegetables and not enough meat can also precipitate the problem. Cheap dog foods, high in fillers and fiber and low in meat, can produce excess gas in a dog's intestines, due to high levels of bacterial fermentation, a process that takes place when lots of carbohydrates are present in the food.

Dogs who are suffering from some type of intestinal disorder or allergic to certain types of foods can also become flatulent. Often this is accompanied by diarrhea, dehydration, and a reduced appetite.

A few dog breeds are more susceptible to flatulence than others. They include Rottweilers, Doberman pinschers, and Dalmatians.

SOLUTION

The first step in minimizing flatulence in your dog is taking him to the veterinarian to eliminate the possibility of intestinal disorders or allergic reactions to a certain type of food. He or she may also recommend a food for your dog, one that will help reduce the formation of gas in the intestinal tract. In addition, certain enzymatic supplements can be effective in reducing the production of gas in dogs. Your veterinarian may prescribe these for your dog, in hopes that they might cure the problem.

Be sure to feed your dog a food that has meat as the first ingredient and not grains or filler material, which can encourage gas in the intestines. Also, eliminate all table scraps from your dog's diet, as these can often accentuate the problem. Try not to change your dog's food if he seems to be doing fine with it. Unnecessary changes in diet can lead to flatulence, as well as diarrhea, so stick with what works.

GARBAGE OR CUPBOARD RAIDING

DESCRIPTION

Some dogs are smart enough to learn how to open a cupboard door to get at the tasty food or garbage hidden inside. A flick of the paw or a nudge with a nose is often all it takes for a determined pooch to gain access to the "mother lode." The owner of such a dog comes home from work and finds refuse all over the kitchen floor or else discovers opened food packages from a pantry closet strewn all over the home, the satisfied dog happily licking his or her chops off in a corner.

WHY YOUR DOG IS DOING THIS

Your dog is a smart, curious creature with a superior sense of smell. If you are gone from the home and the dog is hungry, he will search for something to eat. If his food dish is empty, odds are he will go scouting around the home for something to satisfy his cravings. After checking the countertops, he will soon resort to scenting out something hidden behind a cupboard door. As many people keep their garbage pail in a cupboard under the kitchen sink, that's where their curious pooches head first. Many dogs will figure out how to flick the door open within a few minutes; if the garbage pail has an easily removed lid (or none at all), your pet has hit the jackpot.

Cupboard raiding is common among dogs, particularly smart ones with big appetites. Even dogs who have food readily available to them will often prefer to eat what they can find in cupboards, as the food found there tends to be more aromatic. Given a choice, your dog would probably choose a dish of human leavings over one of dry kibble any day.

Cupboard raiding and garbage theft occur more frequently among dogs who eat only once a day (usually in the evening, when the owner gets home). Because they are hungry throughout the day, their noses often lead them into trouble, often a garbage pail filled with greasy food remnants or a box of cookies behind a kitchen cupboard.

Though normally not dangerous to the dog's health, certain foodstuffs can be potentially life-threatening, Bones from various types of meats can become lodged in your dog's throat or cause a perforation of his stomach or intestines. Plastic or aluminum foil wrapping can also wreak havoc on his digestive system, as can cellophane or large amounts of paper. Chocolate, highly toxic to dogs, can render your pet sick or dead, depending on the size of the dog and the amount eaten. At the very least, garbage and cupboard raiding can disturb your dog's housebreaking habits, leaving you with a disgusting situation to deal with upon arriving home in the evening.

SOLUTION

The solution to this problem is a fairly simple one. First, go out to the hardware store and purchase enough baby cupboard locks to dog-proof all the cupboards in question. Designed to prevent full access to a cupboard or drawer unless a short plastic catch is pushed in and released, these locks will prevent your dog from opening any cupboard or drawer with food or garbage behind it. Installation usually requires a small portable drill and a screwdriver. Once these locks are in place, your dog won't be able to get into the contents of the cupboard and make a mess and possibly ingest something toxic.

In addition to installing the baby cupboard locks, you should make an attempt to limit the amount of garbage you keep in the garbage pail while away. Fragrant items such as leftover steak sandwiches or uneaten bacon should be taken straight out to the garbage can outside the home, so as not to drive the dog crazy with desire. Do the same with the pantry; try not to store food that has a definite aroma or is in an open box or container there.

Make sure your dog is being fed the proper amount of food each day. A dog who is not getting enough food will ultimately go looking for more. In addition, consider feeding your dog two meals a day instead of one. Feeding him a small breakfast before you leave for work might just be the solution to his cupboard thievery.

GROOMING AND HANDLING, AVERSION TO

DESCRIPTION

Some dogs develop a dislike for being groomed and will either run away from or nip the person attempting to do so. Your dog may see the comb or brush and head for the hills or else assume a submissive, defensive posture, with her ears laid back, her tail between her legs. She may struggle, growl, or even physically injure the groomer.

WHY YOUR DOG IS DOING THIS

Several reasons might explain why your dog might not enjoy being groomed. She might have had a bad experience at one time, with the person grooming her accidentally catching the comb or brush in a matted section of her coat, resulting in a painful pull on the skin. Or the dog might have had a groomer try to manhandle her at some point, physically restraining her in order to complete the procedure. As dogs rarely forget an upsetting incident, just one upsetting grooming event can sour her on the procedure forever.

A dog who has had a toenail clipped too short while being groomed will feel a good deal of pain, due to the quick (a blood vessel and nerve bundle running inside the nail) being cut. The quick grows to within a quarter-inch or so of the nail tip; inexperienced groomers often cut it accidentally, causing much bleeding and discomfort. As nail clipping is often included in a grooming session, any dog who has had this occur will fear being groomed.

Any one of several factors could explain why a dog has a low tolerance to handling. If pets have experienced any form of physical abuse in the past, odds are they won't feel very comfortable being handled, even by a caring, gentle owner. A dog who has been teased by children may have similar feelings. Rescue or longtime strays tend to aloof and uncomfortable when being handled, as they have had to struggle to survive and may feel confined or endangered when required to stay in one place for an extended period of time, under the complete control of another. These dogs shy away from handling because they need to feel in control and safe.

Naturally timid or shy dogs will usually allow their owners to handle them but may not be comfortable with guests' trying to do the same. Again, these dogs simply reach a point where they feel pressured, unsafe, or out of control and must then put an end to the handling, even if it feels good.

Some well-adjusted, dominant dogs (particularly unneutered ones) will abruptly decide that they have had enough handling, even though they might have been enjoying the attention right up to the moment of rejection. These dogs seem to genuinely enjoy being touched but quickly reach a saturation point, whereupon they must break off the contact. They reach a point at which the discomfort of the situation overtakes the pleasure of being handling, causing the dog to end the session.

Dogs separated from their littermates before the eighth week may not have received the proper amount of socialization needed to become well-rounded, confident adults. These dogs often shun the physical attentions of others (particularly other dogs). Though normally affectionate with their owners, this type of pet might object to being touched by guests.

SOLUTION

An aversion to being groomed or handled usually stems from either fear or dominance issues, making an easy solution to the problem improbable. The first step, as always, is to try to prevent problems before they arise. First, potential owners should adopt or purchase puppies who have been allowed to stay with their mothers and littermates until at least the eighth week. Doing so will insure that the puppy has learned proper etiquette and socialization skills from participating in mutual grooming sessions with the whole canine family.

Longhaired breeds tend to dislike grooming more than their shorthaired kin, because of the greater chance of tangles or matted hair occurring. It also takes longer to groom longhaired dogs, requiring them to tolerate the procedure for a more extended period of time. Choosing a shorthaired breed will therefore help you minimize the grooming issue, as they take only a few moments to brush out.

Whether you choose a longhaired or shorthaired dog, make sure to begin grooming sessions from the very start of your relationship. Handle your puppy as much as possible during grooming, rewarding her with occasional small treats during the procedure. Begin lightly running a comb through her fur once or twice each day, for a minute or so, again giving her treats during the session. Do the same with a brush. Be sure never to pull too hard, especially if you come across a mat or tangle. Gently work the mat or tangle out with the comb while keeping all tension off the skin. Make the process an enjoyable one, and your dog will become a cooperative pet.

Limit grooming sessions to only a few minutes at a time to prevent your dog from growing bored or stressed. After a few minutes, quit, then reward her with a treat or a play session. Always be upbeat during grooming. Praise and reward her; make grooming seem like a fun game.

If your dog is showing a new dislike for grooming, she might have a sore spot or abscess on her skin. Check for it; if you find something out of the ordinary, see your veterinarian.

If your adult dog simply hates to be groomed but must have it done, consider letting a professional groomer do the job. He or she has plenty of experience in dealing with stressed and unruly dogs and will have the proper equipment and attitude to get the job done. If you do it, odds are your dog will become upset, and possibly he will hold a grudge against you. By allowing a groomer to "take the heat," you avoid damaging your own relationship with the dog. Trimming nails can be an especially risky venture for an inexperienced owner; if you have any doubts about your ability to do so, let a pro do it instead, to avoid damaging the trust you have built up with your dog.

Certain steps can be taken to minimize your dog's aversion to being handled. First, never seek out and force a timid dog to accept handling. When your dog does seem open to being handled, do so gently, taking care not to touch areas that she seems to object to, such as the rump or perhaps the neck or face area. End the handling session while she still seems to be enjoying it as well, to assure that the entire experience is enjoyable for her. Consider rewarding her with an occasional tasty treat during the handling session also, to reinforce and encourage the behavior.

Do not expect your hand-shy dog to accept handling from guests, particularly young children, who can be unpredictable and excessively rough at times. Do allow your guests to offer the dog treats, however; have them place the treat on the floor near their feet, encouraging the dog to come close. Eventually she should allow some minor handling to happen, even if it is limited to brushing up against the person's legs.

To help prevent your dog from becoming hand-shy, make sure to handle her regularly from the first day you bring her home. Always be gentle, and reward a good handling session with a treat or two. Make daily handling a part of the routine. Try to involve guests as well; let them handle the puppy whenever in the home, provided the puppy is not terrified. Teach children to be gentle and to not force the puppy into being handled.

When purchasing or adopting your puppy or dog, be sure she enjoys being handled and stroked before taking her home. Watch her behavior with other dogs and humans; if you see any antisocial behavior, choose another pet.

Never physically punish your dog, as this will probably cool her to handling forever. Any corrections that need to be done should be administered with a leash and training collar. Also, consider having your dog neutered, as doing so will help even out his or her temperament and remove the undesirable effects that hormonal peaks and valleys can have on mood and accessibility.

A dominant dog or one with no obedience training whatsoever will often object to being groomed or handled, as to the dog it seems a form of domination on your part. Your dog must surrender to your manipulations and thus considers them to be challenges to her dominance. These dogs can be a handful to groom or handle and can readily show aggression when pushed. The solution for these dogs is twofold: First, get yourself and your pushy dog into an obedience class right away, to allow you to gain some control and leadership and to take your obnoxious dog down a few notches in the hierarchy. Second, for the meantime, if the dog needs grooming, let a professional groomer do it, without you present. He or she makes a living dealing with uncooperative dogs and won't have much of a problem. Your dog will probably put up a fight, though. Because you do not want her to associate you in any way with the ordeal, try not to be present during the session.

HIDING

DESCRIPTION

Though more common in cats than dogs, hiding can also occur among some canines. Often timid or fearful dogs will disappear under sofas, tables, chairs, beds, or desks whenever anything unexpected happens. The arrival of guests often precipitates the behavior. The hidden dog will normally not reappear until well after the perceived "threat" has left the dog's territory. If made to face the strangers, this dog could become defensive and bite. Anyone reaching into the dog's hiding place risks being bitten.

WHY YOUR DOG IS DOING THIS

This is often caused by profound abuse in the dog's past. Dogs who hide upon the arrival of guests are often strays or rescued shelter dogs, whose previous owners might have beaten them for having repeated housebreaking accidents or for doing damage to the home while they were out. Despite now living with new, loving owners, these dogs find it hard to break with the past.

Other profoundly shy dogs are that way simply due to heredity. If your dog's parents exhibited profound timidity, odds are he will as well.

Some dogs begin to hide whenever loud noises occur, such as those of firecrackers or thunder. Perhaps scared by a loud noise when still a puppy, the dog remembers and shows fear whenever a loud event takes place.

Whether the shyness was caused by heredity or an environmental experience, reserved, cautious dogs often become easily overwhelmed by new persons or situations presented to them. The only way such dogs know to protect themselves is to disappear until the perceived threat is gone.

Some domestic dog breeds are by nature much more cautious and reserved than others. These include many toy breeds, who often worry due to their small stature, as well as sight hounds such as the saluki, Afghan, borzoi, greyhound, and Scottish deerhound, who all tend to act in a more reserved, catlike manner with regard to strangers. Breeds such as the chowchow and the shar-pei tend to be somewhat standoffish as well, as do the Lhasa apso, the puli, the Australian cattle dog, and the soft-coated wheaten terrier. Any of these breeds are capable of going off and finding a quiet spot to occupy until the strangers depart.

Moving your timid dog from her familiar territory to a new, unfamiliar one might also cause her to hide. Being removed from the comfort and security of familiar surroundings to a strange and foreign place can overwhelm some sensitive dogs, who might initially assume that the new place already has established dogs living in and around it, who claim the place for themselves. Being forced to invade another dog's domain can be very stressful to your dog, especially if she tends to be on the submissive side.

SOLUTION

The dog who hides whenever strangers show up obviously feels threatened and may have a strong hereditary component driving the behavior. Because of this, it can often be difficult to modify. You can try, however, by first attempting to desensitize your dog to unpredictable events. Start by leaving a television or radio on while you are gone.

Tune into a station with lots of conversation happening, so the dog can slowly become used to the sound of strange persons talking.

Next, try to limit the number of places your dog can hide when guests come over. Place objects under the sofa and chairs, so that she has no place to hide, and close doors so that she can't run off and hide under a bed or in a closet.

When guests do come over, let them know what you are trying to do and inform them not to seek out the dog but simply sit calmly in one place. Progress can be something as small as having your dog in the same room as the guests without her cowering or growling.

Try putting your timid dog on a regular feeding schedule, instead of free-feeding her throughout the day. This will create definite times during the day at which she will feel truly hungry. By doing so, you will be able to get her to respond to treat offerings more readily, especially right at or before mealtime. In addition, consider ringing a bell whenever you feed her, to condition her to believe that the sound means good things are about to happen. Then, invite a guest over at the dog's dinnertime. Have the guest prepare the food, place it down, ring the bell, then leave the kitchen. If the dog is hungry enough, she will come out of hiding to eat. In this way, you use one strong instinct, the food drive, to supersede another, namely, the fear of strangers. If this is done often enough, your dog will eventually come to see the appearance of a guest as a sign that delicious food is on the way. Realize, however, that she will most likely retain some of her initial trepidation toward strangers and, if pushed too far, could show fear-aggressive tendencies.

If your dog tends to be a shrinking violet, you are probably reinforcing the behavior by cloistering her away from activity. In order to effectively desensitize her to her fears, you need to get her outside, on-leash, within sight of people. Take her for a walk down a street with a few pedestrians in sight and with automobiles going by on a regular basis. The people should not be too close at first and should not be asked to pet your dog. Just let her see activity from a distance. Gradually take her for walks in areas with a good amount of people milling about, such as parks and entrances to malls. Do not allow people to pet her; simply let her see the people walking to and fro. During this, praise her and give her a few treats. By doing so you will slowly and effectively desensitize her to unpredictable activity.

Hiding due to fear of loud noises is very hard to minimize, due to the behavior being so ingrained. About all you can do in this case is avoid comforting your dog when she exhibits the behavior. Doing so can actually reinforce the dog's fearful response. Instead, just let her be for a few minutes, then try to distract her from her fears by pulling out her tennis ball or Frisbee or by shaking a box of dog treats.

HOUSE-SOILING PROBLEMS

DESCRIPTION

House soiling is always a major concern for dog owners, as any canine who fails to eliminate in the proper designated location makes life miserable for everyone in the home. The puppy or adult dog in question may choose to defecate or urinate in an inappropriate spot or spots, possibly ruining carpets, bedding, or flooring. Once a location has been chosen, the pet will often reuse it, further aggravating the owner. The undesirable spot the dog chooses to eliminate in is often a closet, bed, or dirty clothes pile, which provides the errant animal with materials to hide the "mistake" in.

WHY YOUR DOG IS DOING THIS

Many reasons exist to explain house soiling. First, if you have a new puppy, he probably has no concept of what being housebroken means. His mother or breeder cleaned up after him. Now it's up to you to teach him what your expectations are, in your home. If your problem is with a puppy you have had for a few weeks or months, then the reason points to incorrect methods used in trying to housebreak him. Many owners attempt to paper-train their puppies in the home; this classic method works poorly and only encourages the puppy to eliminate in the home. Other owners don't even use the paper and simply try to keep an eye on the in puppies, in hopes of noticing just when they need to go out. This method almost always fails miserably and leads to months of conflict. Others simply scream, yell, and strike their puppies when they have accidents. This is the best way to ensure a puppy will never be properly housebroken.

A newly adopted adolescent or adult dog can often exhibit house-soiling problems. Perhaps used to being an outdoor pet, this dog comes into your home knowing nothing about elimination protocol. If you assume he is housebroken, you will be in for a rude awakening. When you adopt a puppy or an adult dog, you inherit his previous owner's training methods, however good or bad they were. Generally, adopted dogs have to be treated as if they were puppies, with no house-training whatsoever.

The dominant, territorial dog doesn't have "accidents" in the home. He knows exactly what he is doing. Often an unneutered male, this dog is exhibiting classic marking behavior in and around his territory. He is telling you and everyone else that he is the boss, not you. Like wolves in the wild, he is staking out his domain, to let all know of his dominance. If a guest person or dog comes to the home, invariably this dominant terror will lift his leg somewhere to display his power and control.

Sick dogs might temporarily lose control of their bladders or bowels, perhaps symptomatic of the condition. Most dogs come down with an upset stomach or diarrhea sometime in their lives, just as we do. Often the urge to eliminate comes on too soon for the poor pet to get to the proper area in time, causing an accident in the home.

Geriatric dogs often gradually lose the ability to control urination and defecation. Often such dogs will urinate in their sleep and wake up in a small pool of urine. The same can occur with defecation as well. Though often treatable by your veterinarian, this problem usually gets worse, not better.

SOLUTION

The solution to your problem depends, of course, on your unique situation. Let's take these special cases one step at a time.

The New Puppy, or Adopted Dog with Questionable House-training

When bringing a new dog into your home, you should assume that he is not housebroken and that you need to teach him what your expectations are. First, forget about paper training. It only teaches your dog that it's OK to eliminate in the home. Instead, you should take advantage of your dog's instinct to keep his sleeping area (or den) as clean as possible. To do so, you must purchase and use a dog travel crate, available at any good pet store (see instructions for acclimating a dog to a crate, under the section entitled *"Crate, Aversion To"*). When you are not able to directly supervise your puppy or adult dog, he must be in his crate. While he is in it, he will instinctively hold off on urinating or defecating until away from his sleeping area. The new puppy or adult dog must sleep in the crate and be in it whenever you cannot be at home. If you are gone for more than a few hours each day, you need to have someone else come over and let the dog out, to eliminate, to eat, or just to play. Do not get a puppy if you plan on being away from home for many hours during the day. It is not fair to the dog. Get a cat instead. That's what they were made for!

When you are home, the new pet should be within visual range at all times and should not have the ability to disappear into quiet, unoccupied portions of the home. Consider clipping a leash on the dog and tying the other end to your belt loop. As you go about your business, your puppy or adult dog will have little choice but to follow you around. You'll be able to watch him and at the same time bond with him.

Feed your new puppy or dog at regular times. Never free-feed him, as this prevents you from predicting when the dog will need to eliminate. By feeding on a schedule you ensure elimination on a schedule as well. Make sure to provide him with water, except when he is in the crate, as that could encourage urination in it. Don't worry; as long as the dog isn't in the crate for hours and hours, you won't be doing him any harm.

Be sure to take your new puppy or adult dog out to eliminate first thing in the morning. Then feed him, then take him out again. Puppies especially often have the need to go right after eating, so get into this habit to ensure success. Always take your dog out after every meal and right before going to sleep. With a puppy under the age of four months, consider taking him out every hour on the hour, to build the routine and to prevent any possibility of an accident. Also, allow your puppy or adult dog to eliminate right after playing, as the excitement will often stimulate the dog's need to go.

If your new puppy or adult dog does have an accident in the home despite your following the preceding advice, take these steps. If you are home at the time and have witnessed the accident, clip the dog's leash on (or have it on in the home already), bring the dog over to the accident, then *firmly scold the mess* and not the dog directly. Sounds goofy? Maybe. The idea behind it is to let the dog know that feces and urine are both unwanted in the home. If you scold your dog in front of the mess, he could begin to think that the mere act of eliminating is bad, causing him to become stressed or secretive whenever the need arises. Scold the mess, then bring the dog out to a proper location and allow him to eliminate there, if necessary. Try to use a word or phrase to go along with the act; when the dog is in the right spot to go, begin softly saying, "Hurry up," or, "Go on," or, "Get in there," over and over, until he actually goes. Then say, "Good hurry up," or whatever phrase you are using. Eventually you will be able to trigger your dog's elimination with the phrase. He will go on cue for you. How's that for a trick? If you take your puppy or dog out, but he doesn't go, bring him back inside and put him in the crate or else tie his leash to your belt loop. Wait fifteen minutes, then take him out again. Eventually he will go. Praise him verbally when he does, though avoid giving him treats, to prevent him from associating food with elimination, which might cause him to go whenever treats are given in the home.

After following these instructions for a month, you should be able to slowly allow your new puppy or dog to have more and more freedom in the home. Begin allowing him to be in a room away from you for a few minutes at a time, gradually increasing the time as the dog matures. If at any time he backslides and has an accident, however, go back to the crate and/or the leash-on-the-belt-loop technique and start again. Once the dog can go about six weeks without an accident, you have succeeded in housebreaking the pooch.

If your dog has an accident while you are away, use the same technique described before. Put his leash on, take him to the mess, *scold the mess*, then take him outside. Do not stick his nose in it or hit him. That will just make matters worse. Make sure to also clean the mess up thoroughly, using an odor-neutralizing cleaner, available at all pet stores. If the sight has any scent remaining, your dog will home in on it and use it again. Do not allow your dog to actually see you cleaning up the mess, however, as this might make him think that it's OK to for him to play with it. *If you, the leader, can touch it, why can't I?* he thinks.

The Marking Dog

The marking dog eliminates in the home because he wants to and not because he has to go. To prevent marking in the home, you must do the following:

Have your dog neutered, to minimize his domineering, territorial instincts. If your dog is not neutered, face the fact that he will mark in the home from time to time, even if he respects you as his leader. Even unneutered females will mark occasionally; having such dogs neutered will minimize the chances of it happening again.

Attend an obedience class with the offending dog. A dominant dog who marks in your home has no respect for you or the rules. You can change that by learning how to control him and how to restore yourself as the leader of your pack. Once he knows his place and becomes subordinate to you, the marking should stop.

Correct the dog if he marks in the home. First, keep a six-foot leash clipped to the offending dog's collar while in the home. When he does mark, grab the leash, correct him with a few firm jerks, and say, "No!" Put him into a crate for an hour, to think about what he has done. Then let him out and take him directly to an appropriate spot to urinate. If you have been away for hours and discover a wet spot, you should not call the dog to you and then punish him, as this will only teach him not to come to you in the future. Instead, put his leash on, bring him over to the wet spot, scold the wet spot, then take the dog out to an appropriate place to urinate. In addition, you will have to crate the dog whenever you are away and begin basic House-training 101 again, as if he were a puppy. When you are gone, he is in the crate, period. When you are home, he is tied to your belt loop or in the room with you with his leash on. After six weeks without marking, he graduates. In the meantime, he sleeps in a crate, and not in your bed!

The Sick Dog
Never punish your dog for having an accident when he is sick. Take him to the veterinarian for the appropriate treatment, then keep him in a crate at home when you are not around until he is feeling better. If he eliminates in the crate, do not punish him. Simply clean out the crate. Also, don't leave a blanket or pillow in the crate when the dog is ill, as it may become soiled beyond repair.

The Old Dog
Often old dogs will gradually lose the ability to hold it in until no behavioral techniques on the owners' part will have any effect. Most commonly old dogs will lose control of their bladders well before their bowels; this makes cleaning up a bit easier, but it is still upsetting to both you and your pet. He is aware of the problem but cannot help it. If you suspect age is the culprit, take your dog to the veterinarian. Numerous medications exist that can help control incontinence, so do not give up.

If the problem cannot be solved through medication, you may need to create a outdoor dog pen with a concrete floor for your dog. If you live in a region of the country that suffers through cold winters, however, this may be hard on him, unless you can somehow heat the enclosure.

If your dog cannot control his bowels or bladder anymore, it might be time to consider euthanasia. His quality of life is at an all-time low, as is your ability to help.

Though a tough, heart-wrenching decision, it is one you should consider, particularly if he also has joint problems, which often accompany the loss of house-training.

HUMPING

DESCRIPTION

Though humorous to envision, this annoying behavior can be an indicator of more serious behavioral problems. The dog in question (almost always an unneutered male) will attempt to mount another pet, a piece of furniture, or even the leg of a human, whereupon he will simulate coitus for a short period of time.

WHY YOUR DOG IS DOING THIS

A dog who gets into the annoying habit of humping is simply expressing his desire to satisfy his sexual needs, in the absence of an available mate. Many owners insist on keeping their male dogs intact, despite the fact that the pets will never be given the opportunity to breed. When the dog comes of age, strong hormonal drives cause him to seek out sexual fulfillment. When no mate is available, the humping behavior is the only alternative.

The problem with this behavior (besides the embarrassment of a guest suffering the indignity) is that it can point to a lack of leadership and control on the part of the dog' owner, especially if the dog is humping persons in the home, including the owner. Any dog willing to do this to a human being shows a serious dominance problem and must be corrected. A dog this brazen about displaying his dominance probably exhibits other bad behaviors related to dominance, including some form of aggression, marking, food guarding, and a basic lack of obedience. Apart from never being neutered, a dog who displays humping behavior thinks he can do so without retribution, because his owner has never set rules or taken control. Instead, the dog has ruled the roost, for the most part, and is simply expressing that through humping, disobedience, and a number of other behaviors.

SOLUTION

Guess what your first step should be? That's right; pick up the phone and make an appointment with your veterinarian to have the dog neutered! The surgery is painless and quick, and your male dog will no longer have unneeded hormones raging through his body, causing all manner of unwanted behaviors. You don't need to breed him, and you certainly don't want his annoying little habit to go on. You will both be better off.

Having your dog neutered will help remove his need to exhibit the behavior for sexual gratification. He might still perform the behavior, however, if he has been doing it for so long that it has become an ingrained part of his repertoire, a habitual act that is part of his daily ritual. It has also been a way for him to exert his dominance over you and other family members; he thinks himself dominant and will even after being neutered. Therefore, you must remove that idea from his mind by reclaiming the role of leader. To do so, begin by taking an obedience class, to learn the basic skills needed to control your dog. Then change the ways things are done at home. Do not allow him to sleep in bed with you. In fact, banish him from your bedroom entirely. Doing so will immediately take him down a notch or two in the dominance hierarchy. Next, feed him only after you have eaten, as leaders (you) always eat first. Then, make him earn all attention and treats. He has to sit for a pat on the head or a treat. He must lie quietly for a few minutes before being served dinner. Finally, do not allow him to go through doors before you or to pull you down the street while on a walk. Leaders don't follow. Remember that! He should walk nicely by your side and pay attention to you.

After establishing these new rules, clip a leash onto his collar while he is in the home. If he attempts to mount and hump a piece of furniture or a person, grab the end of the leash and give him a firm jerk while saying, "No!" Then put him into his crate (or a darkened room) for thirty minutes. If you do this each time, he will eventually stop the behavior.

IGNORING COMMANDS

DESCRIPTION

Dogs may refuse to respond to a command, despite repeated pleas from their owners. Often in the company of other dogs or in an active outdoor setting your dog may simply ignore the command to "come" and continue to do whatever she pleases, which might involve chasing a squirrel or playing with another dog. It can also occur in the home, however, with little, if any, distraction present, particularly with dominant dogs, adolescents, or older animals.

WHY YOUR DOG IS DOING THIS

Several reasons could explain this behavior. The most likely is that your dog is simply ignoring you because she feels she has better things to do and that you do not have the status to require her to pay attention. Your position in the pack hierarchy is, in other words, lower than you'd like it to be. Thinking herself equal (or superior) to you, she chooses to ignore you until she's done doing what she wants to.

A dog who ignores commands is often an unneutered male, whose sexual desires cause him to put you on the back burner. He may be in search of a female or else be participating in some type of territorial display with another male. Either way, you lose.

Dogs with keen noses might also ignore commands because of very enticing scents that they have just become aware of. Hounds are particularly guilty of this; owners of breeds such as the beagle, basset hound, foxhound, harrier, and bloodhound often compete unsuccessfully for their dogs' attentions, due to their fabulous noses. German shepherds, Doberman pinschers, retrievers, and pointers are also guilty of this biological distraction.

Dogs between the ages of six months and a year are very likely to ignore the commands of their owners. Simply put, these dogs are teenagers, who are feeling pangs of independence and whose sexuality is just beginning to blossom. This makes for a highly distractible dog.

A dog with a hearing problem will often inadvertently ignore a command given without an additional hand gesture. Older dogs generally lose their hearing gradually, and owners often do not take into consideration the dog's reduce capacity to hear, instead thinking their pets are being disobedient. Owners of dalmatians or white German shepherds should also be aware of possible hearing difficulties, as both have a high occurrence of hearing loss. When deafness is hereditary or congenital, the problem will evidence itself right from the start, when the dog is just a puppy. The owner of a puppy who seems not to respond to audible cues (such as loud hand clapping when the puppy is not watching) should see the veterinarian immediately.

SOLUTION

First, if your dog isn't yet neutered, have it done. His or overall behavior will improve tremendously, and he or she won't be distracted by sexual desires. A neutered dog is more likely to respond to commands and will have less of a desire to roam far from home.

If you suspect your dog ignores you due to dominance issues, get yourself and your dog to an obedience class in your area as soon as possible. There you will learn how to control your dog under many circumstances, as well as how to restore yourself as the true pack leader. Once you do this, your dog will want to pay attention.

If you are the owner of a dog with an especially keen nose, she may ignore you from time to time despite being a well-trained and respectful pet. She can't help it, really. To deal with it, first make sure that your dog's obedience is up to par, including the recall or *come* command. Work it regularly, using sporadic treat rewards. Take an obedience class, and practice the recall with other dogs present. Then consider enrolling in a tracking class, where you will learn how to use your dog's amazing nose to track down persons, objects of clothing, toys, or whatever else you decide. By doing so, you get to harness the dog's innate ability to follow a scent and in doing so gain some control over it. Instead of ignoring you to follow a scent on her own, your dog will now work with you to find whatever you ask her to find, using her great sense of smell. This teaches the dog to respond to you even while on the scent. Tracking classes can be found by contacting your local Humane Society or by contacting the AKC and asking for the telephone number of the nearest tracking club. (Note: See Appendix A for contact info on both of these organizations.)

If you suspect that the cause of your dog's disobedience might be deafness, bring her in to your veterinarian, who will help determine if this is the case. If it is, you will need to work with a trained canine behaviorist, who will teach you how to utilize hand signals instead of verbal commands to communicate with your dog. Qualified behaviorists can be found in the yellow pages or by contacting a local pet shelter and asking for a reference.

INCESSANT LICKING, SCRATCHING, OR BITING

DESCRIPTION

The classic image is of a mangy old mutt scratching, licking, and biting himself on the front porch of the old homestead. Hopefully, he's not your dog. If he is, however, he probably has an incessant habit of scratching himself with a back leg or licking and biting various parts of his body in an effort to clean himself or to remove parasites. This often is a habit of dogs who spend much of their time outdoors, as they are frequently less than clean.

Some dogs can develop a habit of incessantly licking at their front paws, despite them being clean, parasite-free, and uninjured. If the licking goes on long enough, open wounds called *lick sores* can appear on the feet.

WHY YOUR DOG IS DOING THIS

Several reasons can explain why your dog might begin incessantly licking, scratching, or biting at himself. First, he may simply be in need of a bath. Though not nearly as fastidious as cats, dogs do like to keep reasonably clean; if yours gets dirty from romping in the mud or swimming in the local pond, he may spend an inordinate amount of time licking himself or scratching from the irritation of the dirt. A filthy coat also tends to become tangled and matted, adding to the dog's discomfort. Or he may have become infested with fleas, ticks, mites, or lice and is frantically licking, scratching, and biting himself in an attempt to get rid of the pests.

A dog with some type of skin disorder such as mange or dermatitis is likely to lick, scratch, and bite incessantly. An injury that causes an open wound in the skin will also cause your dog to lick at it for a prolonged period, in an instinctive desire to clean it and keep it bacteria-free. Even a change of food can cause skin irritation in some dogs, leading to licking and scratching behavior.

Lick sores occur because a dog licks incessantly due to stress. Some situations that can cause stress in your dog's life include:

◆ Physical abuse
◆ Relocation
◆ Recent adoption from a shelter
◆ Loss of a companion
◆ Competition or conflict with another dog
◆ Separation anxiety
◆ Extended periods of isolation
◆ Change to a new food
◆ Serious injury or illness
◆ Severe physical discomfort
◆ Being a breed particularly susceptible to nervousness, such as dalmatians and Dobermans.

Whatever the cause, a dog with chronic lick sores continues to lick at them, making them worse and worse. Often an entire paw can be completely denuded of skin, requiring extensive work on the part of your veterinarian.

SOLUTION

If your dog spends lots of time outdoors, chances are he is either dirty or infested or both. The simplest solution is to bathe him thoroughly, using a veterinarian-approved flea and tick shampoo. Before doing so, brush out any tangles or mats you find in your dog's his coat, as bathing will just make them worse. If your dog's coat is hopelessly matted and tangled, consider letting a professional groomer do the job for you. Though this can be a bit pricey, you will appreciate the results.

If the cause of your dog's licking, scratching, and biting is not a dirty or infested coat, you may need to visit your veterinarian, who will be able to discern if the pooch has some form of dermatitis, mange, or another skin disorder. With a longhaired dog, be sure to look over his skin carefully, to check for any reddened or injured areas. The long coat can often obscure problems from an owner's sight.

If you suspect that your dog is incessantly licking at his front paws due to some type of stress in his life, visit your veterinarian to have the paws treated and dressed. Your dog may need to wear a large "Elizabethan" collar around his neck for a while, to prevent his mouth from reaching and further irritating his feet. The collar looks like a huge lampshade and fits onto the dog's collar.

After checking in with the veterinarian, go through the aforementioned list of reasons for stress and determine if any apply to your dog. Or, use your own intimate knowledge of your pet to deduce the problem. A stressed dog, in addition to having lick sores, may often pant heavily, whine, bark, or pace. Try to remove the cause of your dog's stress. For instance, if you think he is suffering from separation anxiety while you are at work all day, try to have a neighbor or friend come over once or twice while you are gone to take him for a walk. If another dog in the family is causing the stress, work on both dogs' obedience in an attempt to get some canine order back into your little pack. Get them to respect you more, and they will in all likelihood show more respect toward each other. If you cannot identify the cause of your dog's stress, consult with a canine behaviorist, who will be able to discern just what is going on. Your veterinarian will be able to provide you with a referral.

JUMPING ON PEOPLE AND FURNITURE

DESCRIPTION

The dog who typically jumps on people is an active, happy dog who doesn't quite understand proper etiquette. The behavior normally occurs when someone comes into the home; the dog will rush over and jump up, placing his or her front paws upon the person's legs, waist, or chest, depending on the dog's size. Smaller dogs will jump up onto the lap of a seated person and stay there as long as they can.

Jumping up, in addition to being disrespectful, can also be down outright dangerous. A young child or senior citizen could be knocked over and injured or, at the very least, frightened into never wanting to interact with the dog again.

Many dogs will also show a desire to jump up onto a chair, sofa, or bed. Some will blatantly refuse to get off, going so far as to growl or bite if someone attempts to remove them. Toy breeds are especially guilty of this behavior.

WHY YOUR DOG IS DOING THIS

In a litter of puppies, playing stops only for eating or sleeping. They jump all over one another and have a grand old time. The playing has an ulterior motive, however; it allows the puppies to work out exactly where they are in the "pack." The puppy who always wins at wrestling matches is eventually seen by the others as the dominant one, while the perennial loser is normally considered to be the most subordinate. Puppies who allow others to continually jump atop them are, in effect, saying, *"Yes, I am at the bottom of the pack*." The others may love these pups but see them as dogs with little say-so.

If your dog continually jumps on you, family members, and guests, she is doing so not only out of happiness but also out of an innate desire to raise herself up in the pack standings. If you allow her to jump on you without reprisal, you are telling her that she is dominant over you. For this reason, the behavior should not be encouraged. Besides, a dog with dirty paws or long front nails can ruin your clothing!

Dogs who jump up show a clear misunderstanding of where they should be in the pack hierarchy. In the wild, dominant wolves rarely allow subordinates to jump on top of them, except in the case of a playful, naive cub.

A dog who insists on jumping up into someone's lap while he or she is seated is exhibiting an even more dominant form of the behavior. Whenever a dog assumes and maintains a superior position over another dog (usually above it), that dog is plainly exhibiting dominant behavior. Surely, your dog enjoys the stroking and rubbing she gets when parked in your lap. But the fact is that she is initiating the behavior, not you. She has trained you to stroke and groom her just by jumping atop your lap. Who owns who? Some dogs won't even allow you to remove them from your lap without growling or some other form of objection. Most owners don't see the larger picture, however, and readily allow their dogs to jump up into their laps whenever the dogs desire.

By far the worst behavior of this type that you can permit is allowing your dog to sleep in your bed, either with you or alone. The leader of a pack always sleeps in the highest, most desirable spot, sharing it with few, save perhaps his mate. An owner who allows his or her dog to use the bed is clearly communicating to the dog that he or she is at least of equal status in the pack. Besides when your pet eats in relation to you, where she sleeps determines (in her mind) her ranking and her subsequent attitude toward you and the other family members. Toy breeds, often spoiled and pampered by their owners, tend to be allowed into their beds more frequently than larger breeds, perhaps explaining why diminutive dogs, more so than others, regularly exhibit territorial and dominance aggression. They clearly perceive that they have exalted status, due in part to having unfettered access to any bed, chair, lap, or sofa in the home.

SOLUTION

Here is a quick, effective plan to stop a dog from jumping up on you whenever you come into the home. First, from now on, ignore your dog for five minutes before you leave the home and for five minutes after you have arrived. By doing so, you will slowly defuse the greeting and departure rituals and make them both nonevents. Most owners make a big scene when they leave or come home. It usually goes like this: *"Oh Muffy, I'm leaving now, but I'll be back, dear; don't worry; now give Mommy a big kiss and a hug before I go . . ."* Or: *"Oh, Muffy, I missed you so!! It's so good to be back home with you!!! Come give me a big kiss, and jump up on me and tell me how much you care!!"* By getting excited and worked up when you leave or come home, you get your dog worked up as well. She can't help but jump all over you. Instead, just play it cool when you leave or arrive home. Ignore her for a few minutes upon arriving home, until you are ready to calmly greet her. Then do so, with a pat on the head and a casual hello. That's it. When you leave, simply leave, without any long-drawn-out emotional scene. By doing so, you will help keep the dog calm and prevent overexcitement.

If your dog continuously jumps on you when you arrive home, try this. For a medium- to large-sized dog, let her jump up on you, then calmly but firmly grab hold of her front paws and don't let go. Don't pinch them; simply hold onto them firmly. Then simply talk to your dog in a calm voice, about nothing in particular. After about five seconds, she will attempt to pull her paws away from your grasp. Don't let her. Continue to hold on firmly until she really begins to struggle. Then, when she begins to strenuously object, let go while simultaneously saying, *"Off!"* in a firm tone. From now on, whenever she jumps up on you, use this technique. I guarantee she will stop jumping up on you by the third or fourth time.

An alternative method is to keep a leash clipped onto your dog's collar while she is in the home and whenever she approaches you casually step on the leash so that very little slack remains in it. When she attempts to jump up, the leash will stop her in her tracks. She corrects herself, in other words. As long as you have your foot on the leash, she cannot jump on you. By the third or fourth time, she should get the idea. This technique will work for dogs of any size.

If your dog insists on jumping up onto you while you are seated, keep a leash on her in the home. When she jumps up, grab the leash, give it a quick jerk, and say, *"No!"* Then say, *"Off!"* while physically moving her off you with the leash. When she is back on the floor, praise her by saying, *"Good off!"* Use this same method if she attempts to jump up onto a chair, sofa, or bed.

Your dog can be in your lap or in a chair next to you if you desire her to be, but only upon your request. It has to be your desire and not hers. To do so, invite her up by saying, *"OK, Muffy, up!"* while slapping your leg. Then, when you want her to get off, simply say, *"OK, Muffy, off!"* If she doesn't jump off on her own, use the leash attached to her collar to physically move her off.

As far as your bed is concerned, it's a good idea to keep your pet off it, especially if she tends to be a pushy, dominant dog. Simply close the door to your bedroom to keep her out during the day. At night, she can sleep next to your bed, in a crate, or on a comfy rug or doggie bed. If she tries to jump up on you during the night, guide her back off while saying, *"No! Off!"*

If your dog tends to jump up on furniture while you are away, you can try a few tricks to keep her off. First, try putting several long pieces of double-sided sticky tape atop the sofa or chair in question, spaced out at about six-inch intervals. Most dogs hate the sticky feeling on their feet and bodies and will quickly jump off. If that doesn't work, try a few sheets of aluminum foil or even a folding chair or two. Anything that makes it undesirable for her to jump up there. Once you find something that works, keep with it for at least six weeks. By then, you should have effectively stopped her from jumping up.

If she tries jumping up onto the furniture while you are home, simply squirt her in the mouth with water from a water pistol or plant sprayer bottle while simultaneously saying, *"No! Off!"* Try mixing a teaspoon or two of white vinegar into the water for added effectiveness.

KEEP-AWAY AND STEALING

DESCRIPTION

Some dogs love to grab possessions of their owners and play a little "you can't catch me" game, knowing full well that humans can't run as fast as dogs. Such dogs, often a spaniel or retriever, will choose an object such as a sock, shirt, wallet, or something else of yours and taunt you into trying to catch them, running around the home or yard, stopping only long enough to tease you some more. They may also use a ball or toy that the two of you may have been playing fetch with. If you do manage to get hold of the object, often the dog will growl and become extremely possessive over it.

WHY YOUR DOG IS DOING THIS

Part attention-getting ploy and part possessive/aggressive behavior, keep-away episodes can be confusing to an owner, who sees a dog attempting to initiate a playful game while at the same time possibly growling over the issue of who really owns the item in question. The dog acts very much like a dominant puppy in the act of teasing littermates into action. Once the other puppies get close to the item in question, however (perhaps a toy or a bone), this puppy stands his ground, growls, and says, *No, it's mine; I am just messing with you. Leave it alone or I'll clobber you.* In other words, keep-away is symptomatic of playful yet dominant dog, who see the humans in their family not as superiors but as littermates with equal or lesser status.

Often a behavior exhibited by dogs who love to fetch, keep-away can be an annoying game when the item in question is something essential to you, such as a wallet or a set of keys. Often a dog who develops this behavior belongs to a family with one or more young children, who unknowingly reinforce the problem by chasing the dog around the home and in the yard. In the dog world, leaders don't chase but are instead chased. Alpha wolves do not put up with the teasing of subordinate pack members but would simply run them down, discipline them, then take the item in question back. Dogs' taunting people to do so is indicative of their understanding their physical superiority over humans. Such dogs are, in fact, controlling and using their "humans" for their own amusement.

This behavior often leads to problems with dominance and control. A child or an adult might ultimately get bitten when trying to regain the item that the dog has pilfered. In your dog's mind, nothing is wrong; he is simply protecting what is his from his subordinates. If the item is a ball or toy, the dog may be even more protective of it, as it is clearly his possession. In addition, dogs who learn to elude their owners during a chase game will rarely, if ever, obey a *come* command, even if their lives are at stake.

SOLUTION

Dogs who play keep-away with their owners or regularly steal items that do not belong to them have has probably been encouraged to do so at some point in their lives, usually during puppyhood. Children and adults love to chase puppies around the home and thrill in seeing the dogs grab something up off the floor and run around as fast as they can, having the time of their life. Unfortunately, puppies grow up and may become big, fast dogs who can evade even the fastest human with ease. The first way to prevent annoying keep-away games from becoming a real issue is to discourage the behavior from the start. No one in the family should chase the dog, ever, no matter what age. Remember, leaders do not chase. They are chased. If you chase your dog, you lose leadership points and contribute to a future dominance problem. If anything, have him chase you. If he ever attempts to goad you into chasing him, ignore him. Walk away. It will diffuse the situation.

In place of chase games, teach your dog to fetch. Start when he is young, with a ball inside the home. Tease him with the ball, then drop it a few feet away. He will eventually pick it up in his mouth; when he does, immediately begin praising him and calling him back to you. Clap; coo; back away invitingly, whatever works to get him back to you. When he returns, lavish him with praise while cleverly removing the ball from his grasp. Try saying, "Give," while you take the ball from him; then praise him when he surrenders it. Then toss it a few feet farther away and repeat the process. Always stop working on *fetch* while the dog is still hot to participate. Never work a behavior until the dog becomes bored and stops of his own accord. This way, he will be ready and willing for the next session. Gradually lengthen the distance you toss the ball until you can play the game in the yard, with the ball thrown at least fifty feet each time.

To minimize keep-away and stealing in the home, remove from your dog's reach any items he might find desirable—dirty or clean laundry, shoes, wallets, keys, remote controls, or whatever he might have picked up in the past. Do not leave food items on counters or tables, either, as the dog might take them as well. Only leave the dog's toys down on the floor. If he tries to initiate a keep-away game with one of these, simply ignore him. It's no fun if no one else plays.

If your dog still manages to get hold of something of yours, do not chase him, as this will only reinforce the behavior. Instead, keep a leash on him in the home, preferably a line that is at least ten feet long. Have it clipped to his collar. When he begins to taunt you, your car keys in his mouth, simply ignore him, while casually stepping on the end of the long tether. Then, pick it up and reel him in like a trout. When he is directly in front of you, command him to sit (if he knows how), then take the item from him while saying, "Give." If he growls at this point, spray him right in the mouth with a water/vinegar solution. This will almost certainly cause him to drop the item, which you can then retrieve. At this point, do not discipline him, as he might think he is being punished for dropping the item. Simply let go of the lead and ignore him completely for at least thirty minutes. Leave the lead on him in the home for at least six weeks, so to always be ready.

In conjunction with the preceding technique, you should attend an obedience class with your teasing little thief as soon as possible. He has a problem accepting you as his leader and needs to have this corrected. Learning how to control your pet on a daily basis will help put a stop to many domineering behaviors, including keep-away and stealing.

MOUTHING OR BITING

DESCRIPTION

Mouthing or biting can be defined as dogs' using their mouths to get attention, defend themselves, or to stop an unwanted behavior from continuing. Whatever the cause, the use of your dog's mouth on a human being should never be tolerated or rationalized, ever, unless the pet is defending the person from harm.

The instances in which mouthing or biting can occur are nearly unlimited. Either can occur in conjunction with any of the forms of aggression mentioned early in part 2. It should be stated that if your dog is currently exhibiting any serious biting or aggression problems toward you or anyone else, contact your veterinarian immediately. The veterinarian will evaluate the dog for possible physical or emotional disorders and then refer you to an experienced canine behaviorist, who will hopefully aid you in solving the problem. No book can teach you how to deal with such a serious problem. Only years of experience with aggressive dogs can do that. Instead, this section will deal with mouthing and biting problems of a slightly less serious nature, involving untrained puppies or pushy, dominant adult dogs who use their mouths to intimidate or influence. Make no bones about it, though; any signs of mouthing or biting, however playful or harmless they might appear, should be taken seriously and stopped immediately.

Often puppies will mouth their owners' hands during play or to get their attention. If this behavior is not dealt with, the dog will carry it over into adulthood. Or an uninformed owner might actually encourage his or her dog to mouth or play-bite, through roughhousing or play-slapping the dog in the face.

Some dogs learn to control and dominate their owners

simply by using their mouths. For instance, if mouthy dogs no longer desire to be brushed, they might turn and lightly bite groomers' hands. Or if cantankerous puppies decide that they don't want to be held anymore, they might nip at the people holding them, while at the same time struggling to get free.

WHY YOUR DOG IS DOING THIS

If the dog in question is a young puppy, chances are he has just left his litter, where he did plenty of mouthing and play-biting with his siblings. Upon coming into your home, he may think that the same behavior can be applied to you. Accordingly, the dog may play-bite on your hand or clothing. It's normal behavior; you just need to teach him that it is now inappropriate. You are not a littermate; you are the master.

Some adult dogs never learn to stop this puppy like mouthing and play-biting, because many owners just don't know how to train them not to do so or else think the behavior normal or endearing. Gradually, such dogs learns that they can influence you and others simply by using their mouths. This type of behavior in adult dogs indicates a serious leadership problem in the "pack." These dogs think they are of equal or superior status to the humans in the family and as such can discipline them every now and then with a nip. If left uncorrected, this can lead to serious behavior problems and to actual injury.

SOLUTION

Your new puppy needs to learn that the same biting behavior he got away with while among his siblings is not applicable to humans. If your puppy is under four months of age, here is what to do: When he begins to mouth you, grab him firmly by the scruff of the neck and give him a few shakes while simultaneously saying, *"No!"* in a growlish type of voice, much as his mother would do if he did it to her. Then put the puppy down and ignore him for a few minutes. Then pick him up again and pet him around the face and mouth, in an attempt to illicit the biting response. If he does it again, repeat the scruff shake and ignore him again for a few minutes. Upon trying it for a third time, you should see a marked difference in behavior. He may try it again, but without much tenacity or verve. If you use this technique whenever the puppy mouths you, he should get the message quickly. If he doesn't and actually increases his attacks on you, the puppy may have a genetic predisposition toward aggression or may be an extremely dominant animal. If you see no improvement, contact the breeder or your veterinarian. Serious signs of lasting aggression in a dog this young could spell disaster; you may need professional help or a different puppy.

Don't try the scruff shake technique with your dog if he is older than four months. If he is still biting and mouthing at this age, it means he's had time to solidify the behavior and it will be harder to eliminate. Trying the scruff shake at this stage could get you seriously injured. Instead, administer the correction with a leash clipped to a training collar (usually the traditional chain slip collar). While you are petting him around the muzzle, if he shows any desire to mouth you, immediately give him a quick jerk on the leash while simultaneously saying, "No!" in a firm voice. Some trainers will also scream at the moment the dog begins his mouthing; you can try this, as it tends to shock the dog into ceasing the behavior. After giving the dog the leash correction, walk him around for a few minutes and give him a few commands such as, *"Sit,"* or, *"Come."* This will help establish you as being in no mood for any nonsense. Then repeat the petting that initiated the original mouthing. If he again mouths you, repeat the procedure. Continue repeating this procedure until he ceases the mouthing while being petted. When he tolerates being touched without mouthing, praise him lavishly, perhaps giving him a treat or two.

If the biting/mouthing habit is well established, you may need to seek out a skilled canine behaviorist for expert help, especially if your dog is large or has bitten seriously in the past. In the meantime, any dogs showing this type of behavior toward humans obviously have a serious dominance problem and need to have most of their freedom and privileges suspended until the behavior improves. This means such a dog should

- ◆ Sleep in a crate.
- ◆ Wear a leash in the home, so you can correct him immediately after a transgression.
- ◆ Be ignored when attempting to get your attention.
- ◆ Be made to earn attention, food, and respect by obeying any command given to him.
- ◆ Be disciplined for any biting, mouthing, or disobedience, then isolated for an hour in a travel crate, located in a darkened room.
- ◆ Work on basic obedience several times a day.
- ◆ Always be made to wait at a door until you go through first.
- ◆ Always eat after you.
- ◆ Never be allowed to beg for food.
- ◆ Be denied the opportunity to play without first showing a respectful attitude.
- ◆ Have no contact with small children.

All these restrictions are tough but necessary if you are to become dominant in his eyes. Until that happens, he will continue to use his mouth to influence others.

If the biting or mouthing of your adult dog seems coupled with profound aggressive tendencies, run, don't walk, to the nearest canine behaviorist for an evaluation. If your dog growls, sneers, charges, or breaks the skin with a bite, get help. Your veterinarian should be able to refer you. *Do not attempt to deal with it yourself*, as you or the dog could get seriously injured.

OLD AGE, BEHAVIOR PROBLEMS RELATED TO

DESCRIPTION

Dogs are living longer and longer these days. A twelve- or thirteen-year-old canine used to be ancient; now dogs routinely live as long as sixteen or more years, due mostly to better medical care and healthier foods. Often a ten-year-old dog will appear no worse off than one half that age. Only in the final few years of life do dogs begin to show distinct signs of the aging process. Your dog older might become more irritable, particularly toward other pets. She may not respond to your calls as quickly, due to progressive hearing loss. Cataracts may blur her vision somewhat, causing her to miss visual cues. Her reflexes will be slower, as will her strength. A jump that used to be child's play to her five years earlier now becomes impossible, due to stiffer joints and weaker muscles. She may vocalize more due to aches and pains and may want to spend more time indoors if she has access to the outside. Older dogs will often seek out the warmest spot in the home and stay there. Your dog's coat might become drier and less dense and her skin flakier. An older dog (especially a male) might have trouble assuming the proper posture for elimination, due to weaker hips and knees. Your older dog may become heavier due to a slowing metabolism. Her teeth may also begin to fall out. Last, your older dog's house-training habits could take a turn for the worse, due to an aging digestive tract.

WHY YOUR DOG IS DOING THIS

Quite simply, she is, as are all of us, getting older. The aging process slowly but surely takes its toll on the canine metabolism and organ systems. Cells that once renewed themselves easily no longer do so. Senses dull and joints may become stiff and painful from the onset of arthritis. Poor circulation causes her to seek out warmer areas of the home. A slowing metabolic rate causes her to gain weight, despite no increase in food intake. Flexibility is down, causing her to attempt less canine acrobatics. Fetching her favorite ball becomes difficult, if not impossible. Failing organs make her more susceptible to infectious diseases and tumors. As her liver and kidneys decline, urinary tract problems can arise.

Obviously, none of this your dog's fault. When we reach our seventies and eighties, we may be cranky, difficult, and frail, too. Your aged dog who loses patience with a child or another pet is only expressing her frustration at not being able to deal with life the way she used to. House-training accidents rarely are caused by behavioral problems at an advanced age, but are usually physiological in nature instead. You cannot modify the behavior, only work around it by altering the dog's environment to suit the problem.

SOLUTION

Until someone discovers how to reverse the aging process, we won't have many successful methods available for correcting undesirable behavior in the aged dog. Several techniques can be implemented, however, to minimize age's effects on your dog's behavior and well-being, including:

◆ Increasing visits to your veterinarian to monitor the aging process more closely and catch serious problems (such as diabetes or cancer) as soon as possible.

◆ Close eye monitoring of the dog's appetite and weight in order to prevent obesity, tooth and gum problems, and problems with digestion. Dietary changes could be necessary to ensure proper nutrition.

◆ Increasing grooming sessions to keep her coat in good condition. Using a coat conditioner after a bath will help, as will the addition to her diet of two eggs per week and a teaspoon of olive oil per day.

◆ Avoiding the introduction of new pets into your aged dog's home, which might annoy her and perhaps cause her to stress or overexert herself. Try introducing her to a potential pet first, to see if she is accepting of it.

◆ Bringing her into the home on a full-time basis to keep her warm and to prevent injury and infection. The older dog's immune system is not nearly as efficient at fending off contagions. Bringing her into the home and out of the cold, wet backyard will also slow down the advance of arthritic symptoms.

◆ Starting a program of gentle massage to help loosen up stiff joints and muscles and increase circulation.

◆ Regular gentle exercise to delay the aging process. A five-minute play session each day can be all it takes.

OVERACTIVE BEHAVIOR

DESCRIPTION

Overactive dogs seem to be "on" all the time. They are constantly moving, investigating, pestering people, and getting into all manner of trouble. Owners of this type of dog often cannot get a moment's peace; such pets are always underfoot, almost as if someone had been secretly giving them coffee instead of water. Such dogs often demand attention and crave as much exercise as you can give them.

WHY YOUR DOG IS DOING THIS

Several factors can cause a dog to act in an overactive manner. First, the breed of the dog should be taken into consideration. Certain breeds tend to be much more active than others. Those known to be on the active side include:

- All pointers
- All retrievers
- All setters
- Most terriers
- All spaniels (except toys and the clumber spaniel)
- American Eskimo dog
- American and English foxhound
- Australian cattle dog
- Australian shepherd
- Beagle
- Border collie
- Boxer
- Dalmatian
- Doberman pinscher

- German shepherd
- Miniature pinscher
- Pug
- Visla
- Weimaraner

Any dog can be potentially overactive, however; this list is simply to give you an idea of those breeds most inclined to be on full throttle most of the time.

Another possible cause of overactive behavior could simply be that the dog has not yet matured fully. Puppies and adolescent dogs always have a much higher activity level than do mature adults. Once your dog reaches ten to twelve months of age, however, he should begin to slow down a bit.

An unneutered dog will have a higher activity level than a neutered one, driven by hormones. Once unneutered dogs reach sexual maturity, they will want to get out and find mates. Barring them from doing so will result in restlessness, as well as a host of other undesirable behaviors, including destructive behavior, excessive vocalization, and marking.

Switching dogs over from life in the yard or a kennel to an indoor/outdoor lifestyle can also result in restless overactivity, as they had been used to a much larger territory, with many more stimuli to keep them amused. Limited to the home during the day, this pet will for a time appear to be overactive. The same is true for strays and rescued dogs, who often come from outdoor situations.

Diet can play a role in the activity levels of some dogs. For instance, certain commercial dog foods, particularly ones in the "semimoist" category, contain high amounts of sugar, which can cause hyperactivity in animals and humans. Too much protein in the diet can have the same effect. Though dogs do require high levels of protein, too much can raise metabolism and also stress the kidneys.

Boredom and isolation can be a big cause of overactive

behavior in dogs. Leave your dog alone all day with little to amuse himself with and he might start bouncing off the walls for entertainment. When you do finally come home, he can't seem to leave you be; you become the target for all of his pent-up frustrations. It appears to you or others that he is overactive when, in fact, he is just releasing anxiety.

SOLUTION

First, if you prefer a less active dog, try not to acquire one of the aforementioned breeds, as they do tend to be filled with energy. Stick with a good old-mixed breed shelter dog or breeds that tend to be a bit more laid back. Some laid-back breeds include:

- ◆ Sight hounds (though they do need regular running sessions)
- ◆ King Charles Cavalier spaniel
- ◆ Chihuahua
- ◆ Clumber spaniel
- ◆ Maltese
- ◆ Saint Bernard
- ◆ Scottish terrier
- ◆ Shih Tzu
- ◆ Silky terrier
- ◆ Yorkshire terrier

Again, there are exceptions to every rule; certainly some dogs of other breeds can be as laid back as these. These tend to be statistically calmer, however, or at least more controllable by an owner without lots of spare time on his or her hands.

If your hot rod dog is still under a year in age, give him a little more time to mature. He should begin to slow down enough to make the relationship more rewarding. Try not to discourage your puppy to slow him down, as active, curious play is vital to his development.

If your overactive dog has not been neutered, now might be a good time to take care of that. All of that pent-up sexual energy has no place to go; by neutering him you relieve him of the stress. He will be calmer and happier.

If your outdoor-only dog has just been switched over to indoor living, try to give him time to adapt to the smaller territory. Make the home a fun place to live in by putting some toys down and by supplying him with a travel crate for in the home, which he will go to for rest and security. Hide a few tasty treats around the place also, to make things interesting. Doing so will help him readjust more quickly. Though it may take as long as two or three months for him to calm down and accept the new arrangement, it is well worth doing, from a safety and health standpoint.

The same goes for a bored, isolated dog; make the home more interesting. Redirect all of your dog's unspent energy at toys and by training him and taking him for walks. Leave a radio or television on while he's home alone. If possible, have a friend visit for five minutes during the day while you are at work. Whatever works to relieve your dog's boredom will also help slow him down.

Try not to feed your dog any food high in sugar, as this can result in overactivity and poor overall health. Also, check the protein content of his food with your veterinarian to ensure that it isn't too high.

OVEREATING

DESCRIPTION

Many dogs become so enamored of food that their increased weight begins to affect their health. Obese dogs are much more common now than they were a few decades ago, due partially to more dogs living in urban environments, where running and romping in the fields cannot occur. The more pampered your dog is, the better chance of his becoming spoiled and overweight.

WHY YOUR DOG IS DOING THIS

Simple answer: look in the mirror! That's right; your dog's eating habits are completely governed by you. She cannot open the refrigerator and pull out a snack any time she wants one. You have to provide her with food. Thus, any weight gain she shows (except those due to a hormonal imbalance) is because of your actions.

Owners who free-feed run the risk of teaching their pets to eat a little bit of food many times a day. As most owners tend to top off the dish whenever it looks low, dogs who free-feed runs the risk of eating much more than they actually need. Over the course of a few years this can result in obesity.

Another big cause of overeating among dogs is treat giving. Whether prompted by begging or meted out randomly, treats can add up over the course of a day and result in obesity. A spoiled dog who receives treats and table scraps throughout the day learns to expect them and becomes conditioned to the regular offerings. Consumption of such a dog's regular food rarely goes up, however, because it simply does not taste as good as the scrumptious tidbits coming from your plate or the refrigerator.

Sometimes a dominant dog will steal food from a submissive canine (or feline) housemate without the owner knowing. Through intimidation, your imposing dog will eat her food as well as her poor submissive counterpart's before you even notice. This often happens when a new pet is brought into an established dog's domain. The new dog or cat loses weight while the dominant dog gains.

Infrequently a dog will suffer from an underactive thyroid gland. Called *hypothyroidism*, the condition slows down such pets' metabolism, causing their bodies to burn fewer calories, even though they still are eating the same amount of food as usual. Though the metabolism is slowed down, their appetite remains the same, causing weight gain.

SOLUTION

Take your dog to the veterinarian for a checkup. He or she will determine if the dog has a thyroid imbalance. If she does, the condition can be corrected through medication. Your veterinarian will also determine how overweight your dog is and what her target weight should be. Most will also offer helpful feeding tips and can sometimes suggest a different, lower-calorie food to feed your dog.

Create a regular feeding schedule. By doing so you will be able to determine exactly how much food your dog is eating each day. Once that is known, you can then cut her food by 10 or 15 percent in an effort to get her back down to a reasonable weight. A regular feeding schedule will also stabilize her appetite; you will be better able to predict just when she will be hungry. By knowing that you can feed her an exact amount at an exact time, instead of randomly filling and refilling a dish all day, never knowing exactly how much food the dog is really eating.

Your overweight dog should not be receiving treats and table scraps throughout the day, no matter how she begs or how much you enjoy giving them to her. Excess treats will add up and create an obese pet, who will in turn live an average of five years less than a dog at or near his or her ideal body weight. Do not encourage begging by giving treats, especially while you are at the dinner table. The only time to give treats is when you are teaching a new behavior to your dog and you need to reward her. That's it. Remember: if you love her, cut out the spoiling! If she has already learned to beg, teach her that the behavior is not appropriate by spraying her with your trusty plant sprayer bottle while saying, *"No!"* Eventually she will get the idea. Also, make sure that all family members refrain from feeding her extra tidbits. The behavior won't change unless all family members participate.

If one of your dogs is gaining weight while the other is losing, odds are the chunky one is eating the thin one's food while you are not looking. Try supervising them at dinnertime to prevent this. Make sure to have separate dishes located on opposite sides of the kitchen. Watch them to see if theft is actually happening. If it is, simply feed them in separate rooms.

Weigh your overweight dog once a week to chart her weight gain or loss. If she is a small dog, pick her up, weigh both of you, put her down, then weigh yourself. Then subtract your weight from the combined weight to determine hers. If she is a large dog and cannot be lifted by you, try to find someone who can lift her or else stop in at the veterinarian's office at least once a month and ask if you can weigh your dog on their walk-on scale.

Once you have your dog at the weight your veterinarian prescribed, make a real effort to keep her there. Be exact with the amount you feed her. Over a year or two, as little as an extra cup per day can add up to five or ten extra pounds. For most dogs, that's a huge increase.

PILL-TAKING, AVERSION TO

DESCRIPTION

Though more compliant than cats, dogs can be difficult to administer pills to. The resistant dog will often squirm, try to escape, or even bite in an attempt to avoid the procedure. If successful in his attempt to escape, your dog will hide from you and may avoid physical contact with you for quite some time.

WHY YOUR DOG IS DOING THIS

Most dogs are not comfortable about having their feet and mouths messed with, as these are both sensitive and vital to a dog's survival. Your dog may not want anyone (including you) to intrude past his comfort zone. Most dogs consider having someone's fingers jammed down their throats an invasion of their personal space, as would most of us. Some level of resistance is therefore to be expected from your dog during this procedure, especially if you have never tried it before. That said, some dogs will put up more of a fight than others. A dominant, pushy, controlling animal will be far less likely to tolerate being given a pill than a more compliant, submissive pet.

SOLUTION

There may be times when you must administer a medication to your dog in order to help him recover from an illness. It therefore becomes vital to be able to medicate him in some way. Fortunately, many medications are available in powder form, which can simply be sprinkled onto a spoon of canned dog food and given to the dog at mealtime. Any medication in capsule form can also be opened up and sprinkled onto food. Even many solid pills can often be crushed into a powder and mixed into food. If using this method, make sure that the dog is hungry to ensure that he will eat all of the canned food offered.

The best way to ensure that your dog will take a pill when needed is to train him from puppyhood to do so. First, make sure that you handle the puppy from the very first day, including grooming as well as a daily inspection of his body, paws, ears, and mouth. After each handling session, always give him a treat as a reward. After you have

accustomed him to regular handling, you can begin to practice the pill-giving technique. Try it at first with a canine
vitamin or with no pill at all, just to get the technique down.
The technique is as follows:

1. Hold the pill between the thumb and index
   finger of one hand.
2. Place your other hand atop your puppy's head.
   Put the thumb and index finger of this hand into
   the corners of his mouth, hooking them in
   slightly, so that the fingertips are in past the
   molars.
3. Tilt his head back until his nose points straight
   up. His mouth should now open wide enough to
   accept a pill.
4. Quickly place the pill onto the back-center
   portion of the puppy's tongue.
5. Close his mouth and hold it closed for a few
   seconds while gently massaging his throat. This
   will ensure that he swallows the pill.

With practice, you will get very fast at performing this
technique. Don't try this with adult dogs who don't tolerate
handling very well, however, as they could panic. A compliant adult dog shouldn't object too strenuously, though,
provided your technique is fast and effective.

An alternative to actually putting the pill into your dog's
throat is sticking the medication into a juicy food item, such
as a piece of chicken or soft cheese. As long as the dog is
capable of eating it quickly, this should work. It may not
work with small dogs, however, as they may take more
time to eat a treat large enough to hide a pill, often dropping
it to the floor and gnawing on it for a few minutes. When
this happens, they often discover the pill, which falls out
and is left on the floor.

If all else fails, you can go to your pet store and purchase
a "pill gun," which will quickly and painlessly shoot the

pill back into the dog's throat. Whatever technique you use, be sure to always reward the dog afterward with a treat and praise.

PLANT EATING

DESCRIPTION

Many dog owners enjoy keeping houseplants in the home. Unfortunately, some dogs develop a habit of munching on the plants, much to the dismay of the owners. Even those in the garden outside can often fall prey to the veggie-loving canine. Young plants especially, with their tender, succulent shoots, can often fall victim to these vegetation-curious pets. Unfortunately, this annoying behavior can also be potentially dangerous for your dog, as many house- and garden plants are quite toxic to canines. The list of toxic plants includes:

- Azalea
- Bean plants
- Cactus
- Crocus
- Daffodil
- Dieffenbachia
- Hemlock
- Hydrangea
- Ivy
- Lily
- Marijuana
- Mistletoe
- Mushrooms
- Narcissus
- Nightshade
- Oleander
- Philodendron

- ◆ Poinsettia
- ◆ Potato leaves
- ◆ Rhododendron
- ◆ Tobacco
- ◆ Tomato leaves
- ◆ Walnuts
- ◆ Yew

WHY YOUR DOG IS DOING THIS

Though dogs are by and large carnivores, they do sometimes consume vegetable matter, especially in the wild, when dogs consume their prey's stomach and all that is contained inside. Stomach contents of prey animals usually include partially digested vegetable matter, which, when eaten by dogs, can provide them with vitamins and minerals not necessarily found elsewhere.

Some domestic dogs seem to love chewing on and eating plants; why is not completely clear. Several reasons could explain the behavior, however. They may be instinctively searching for nutrients not provided to them in their regular diets. Or some dogs may feel the need to vomit up something disagreeable and eating enough plant material can have this emetic effect on them. Another possible reason for the plant munching is simply that they like the taste and texture of what they are eating. Just look at the canine obsession for chewing on grass when in a field.

SOLUTION

Clearly this behavior should be minimized, not only for the sake of the pretty plant but for the safety of the dog as well. The first step to take is to avoid purchasing plants known to be toxic to both dogs and cats. Houseplants such as the philodendron, dieffenbachia, and ivy, so common in many households, should be either avoided or hung from the ceiling in such a way as to completely prohibit access by the dog. If your dog has access to the outdoors, be sure to avoid all the toxic shrubbery and garden plants listed earlier. Unfortunately, you won't be able to determine your neighbor's planting. This makes it imperative for you to prohibit unsupervised roaming by your dog.

Locate whatever nontoxic houseplants you do have up off of the floor, either in tall stands or from hanging mounts. Plant pedestals should be as high as is practical, to get the plants away from the dog's nose level. Never keep any plants on the floor or anywhere within easy dog access.

Cover the soil of the plant with marbles or rocks to discourage digging. Also, consider wiping down the plant leaves with a diluted soap-and-water mixture; it won't hurt the plant, and it will taste terrible to the dog. You can also purchase a veterinarian-approved dog repellent and apply it to the plant.

Also try placing double-sided tape around the area where you keep your plants in an effort to dissuade your dog from going near. Try aluminum foil strips as well. In severe cases, place mousetraps *underneath* multiple sheets of newspaper around the plants. When sprung, the traps will slap harmlessly into the paper, making a loud sound but not harming the dog. Be sure not to place the traps atop the newspaper, however, as your dog could be seriously hurt. If you can catch the dog in the act of chewing on a plant, spray her with water from a plant sprayer bottle while saying, *"No! Leave it!"* in a stern voice.

Last, try to keep your dog's environment as stimulating as possible to prevent boredom, one of the main causes of improper behavior. Providing lots of toys and other objects to investigate, as well as plenty of play time with you, should keep her nose out of your houseplants.

PULLING WHILE ON THE LEASH

DESCRIPTION

Dogs who pull like tractors while on the leash will strain to be as far ahead of their owners as possible, rarely paying any attention to them during much of the walk. These dogs may mark often or sniff their way down the street, scenting all of the other dogs who have gone the same route that day. If your dog is large and strong, *often* he can physically pull you to the ground or else pull the leash from your hand.

WHY YOUR DOG IS DOING THIS

This is normal behavior for an untrained dog, as most canines will attempt to lead you around, if given the chance. In their world, those who lead always go first; by pulling out in front at the end of a taut leash your pet is telling you that he is in charge of the walk, not you. It's his dance, and he's leading. Often dominant, pushy pets, dogs who pull on the leash get away with it usually because the owners think that's what all dogs are supposed to do. In reality, by allowing the behavior you reinforce your dog's idea that he is running the show.

SOLUTION

One of the first things an owner learns in obedience class is how to stop his or her dog from pulling on the leash during a walk. Here's how to do it. First, purchase a metal slip collar (once called a choke chain). Be sure it fits properly; if in doubt, have the pet store employee fit your dog properly. Also purchase a strong six-foot leash. Leather ones won't hurt your hand at all, though some fabric leashes will also work. Do not use a chain leash, as the metal will bite into your hands when you give the dog a corrective jerk.

Clip the leash to the collar and take your dog to the largest quiet room in your home. Don't go outside yet; you are not ready for that. Now, begin walking in a straight line with the dog on your left side. As you begin, say, *"Bobo, heel."* Keep the leash as loose as possible; a large bow in it should be evident. Take two or three steps, then quickly reverse direction 180 degrees. Do it as quickly as possible, so that your dog is caught unawares. If he makes a quick turn and continues to walk with you, praise him. If not, give him a quick corrective jerk while simultaneously saying, *"No, heel."* The corrective jerk should be a fast horizontal snapping for the leash and not a slow pull upward. Make it as quick as possible and not too hard, but just enough to get his attention. Whenever your leash begins to become taut, reverse and correct. Also, try to keep moving all the time; don't stop to give the corrective jerk. Continue to slowly walk back and forth, correcting your dog if he is not turning with you. Work this until he begins to get the idea and stays close by your side. If at any time he begins to pull out ahead of you, reverse direction while simultaneously correcting him and saying, *"No! Heel."*

Once you perfect this indoors, take it into a quiet backyard. Use the same technique; as soon as your dog begins to pull out ahead, correct him and reverse direction. Remember to keep slack in the leash when not correcting the dog. If you tighten up on the leash, your dog doesn't need to pay attention to you anymore; the tension in the leash tells him where you are and what you are doing. If you keep a loose leash while walking, your dog must pay attention to you in order to know what you are up to. Eventually he will have to start paying attention to you and where you are going to avoid the correction. That is the secret; the dog must now understand that it is *your walk,* not his, and that he is just along for the ride. You can help him keep his position by randomly offering him a treat with your left hand. Hold it at waist level, even with his nose. This will encourage him to walk by your side.

Once you perfect this, take him for a walk down the street. Use the same "reverse and correct" technique any time he begins to pull ahead. Eventually he will get the picture.

If your dog is large and very strong and you are not up to the physical efforts of this exercise, go to the pet store and purchase what is known as a "face collar." These fit a dog much in the same way a bridle fits a horse (though without a bit). Once the collar is fitted to your dog, you clip your leash to the metal ring hanging below his muzzle, and off you go. No matter how strong a puller he is, a face collar will allow you to easily control him with just one hand. The reason is simple: control the head and you control the whole animal. Can you imagine trying to control a horse with a leash and neck collar? That's why a bridle must be used. The same goes for a big, strong dog. Using technology instead of brawn can help solve the problem. If you choose to use a face collar, however, be sure to acclimate your dog to it gradually, as often they dislike the feeling of it on their faces. Allow him to wear it for a minute or so the first day, then lengthen the time until he can wear it for an hour with no objection. Then use it to walk him.

PUSHY OR RUDE BEHAVIOR

DESCRIPTION

Some dogs like to get into the middle of everything. Try to sit down and read a book, and your dog immediately nudges your leg or tries to jump into your lap, seeking your attention. Or try to give a little attention to another pet in the family, and your pushy dog immediately gets in between you and the other animal, insisting that you pay attention only to him. Pushy, obnoxious dogs seems to think that the entire world revolves around them. They can't bear to be ignored and act in a dominant fashion toward all other members of the home (including humans). Such dogs insist on greeting, eating, and investigating first and being the first one in and out of doors. In a nutshell, your pushy, rude dog thinks he is king of the castle.

The overly loving, affectionate dog can also become a bother at times, due to a constant need for self-affirmation and an inbred desire to please humans. Rather than being driven by dominance, this *"pet me, love me, fulfill me"* attitude can often be caused by mild insecurity. Dogs like this often also suffer from separation anxiety when the owner is gone.

WHY YOUR DOG IS DOING THIS

In a very real way, domestic dogs remain in an adolescent frame of mind all their lives. By taking responsibility for your dog's food, shelter, security, and entertainment from puppyhood on, you prevent him from fully maturing, at least in a psychological sense. In a sense, your dog remains forever a teenager.

Nevertheless, he still maintains all of the instincts inherent in a dog, including the desire to establish some level of control over his environment. Each dog possesses an inherent degree of dominance, in comparison to other pets and humans. Some simply think more of themselves than others and go about expressing that quality in their everyday lives. So, imagine, if you will, a particularly dominant dog, forever frozen within an adolescent mind-set. Together these two ingredients make for a pushy, in-your-face pet.

Another cause for pushy behavior in a dog can be breed-related. Certain breeds simply desire more attention than do others. Most golden retrievers, for example, are constantly seeking out attention and acceptance. Bred to interact closely with humans as loyal hunting dogs, this breed can't help but be in your face all of the time, albeit in a loving way. Breeds designed to do their jobs independently of humans (such as herders, guard dogs, far-ranging hunters, and sled dogs) tend to have a more independent mind-set and often do not need constant attention paid to them. A greyhound, bred to track and run down fast-moving game, did so away from the direct control of humans and didn't develop a need for constant supervision and praise. Arctic breeds such as the Siberian husky and the Malamute, bred to spend hours pulling a sled, did so without much input from the musher, who stood back in the sled, often more than fifty feet away from some of the toiling dogs. After a hard day's pull, these dogs would huddle together for warmth, instead of inside a small warm enclosure used by the human musher. They did their jobs, rested, and socialized without much direct input from people. Consequently, most Arctic breeds maintain a cavalier, independent mind-set, rarely plying their owners for excess attention.

Some dogs learn to become pushy and obnoxious through the unintentional actions of their owners. For instance, if your young puppy happens to jump onto your leg during your dinnertime, what will he learn if you not only allow the behavior but also reward it with a tidbit from your dish? Or what would your dog learn if every time he jumped on you you petted him lavishly, then got up to feed him dinner? By doing so, you can take a normal dog and turn him into a pushy brat, who knows that he can get what he wants just by vocalizing, jumping up, nagging, or bullying you in some way, much as a spoiled child might do in the supermarket when wanting his parent to buy him some candy. The parent who gives in just to avoid a tantrum from the child only serves to reinforce the obnoxious behavior.

SOLUTION

Try not to encourage unwanted behavior, right from the start. If your puppy begins to jump on you when he isn't allowed to, say, "*No! Off!*" in a firm voice. If he continues to do so, give him a squirt of water from your trusty spray bottle. Above all, do not reward any behavior you think undesirable; the last thing you should do when your dog becomes pushy is give him a pat on the head or a treat.

Sometimes consistently ignoring a dog's unwanted behavior will be enough to put a stop to it. For instance, if your dog sits in front of you while you are reading and begins to paw at you or bark in an attempt to get you to feed him or let him out, completely ignore him and see what happens. Eventually he should give up and walk away. He may try it again several times, but if each time you ignore him, odds are the behavior will stop, because it isn't being encouraged in any way. Try this if the pushy behavior isn't unbearable or too serious. Remember, never allow your dog to initiate a behavior. Doing so teaches him that he has control over you, one sure path to dominance. You need to initiate, just as any good leader would.

Another technique that can work well on the pushy dog is redirecting the behavior. Often your dog may appear pushy or troublesome due to sheer boredom, or a lack of attention on your part. Instead of waiting for the dog to behave in an undesirable manner, try giving him something to do that will satisfy his need for stimulation. Buy a fun toy at your local pet store and use it to stimulate your dog at least three or four times a day. Leave a few toys down on the floor while you are gone. Get him a travel crate for the home, so he has a place to call his own inside your "territory." Randomly hide treats around the home, to get his attention off you.

Last, be sure to train your dog, to give his mind something to think about other than you and food. Obedience training gives your dog rules and purpose and enables him to better fit into your lifestyle. Plus, having good control over your dog will increase your dominance over him, further minimizing the chance of him becoming pushy or domineering.

RUNNING AWAY

DESCRIPTION

Running away is a somewhat different behavior from escaping. Often owners take their dogs to a park, then take them off the leash in order to play fetch or to let them simply stretch their legs and run. When the leash comes off, many dogs take it as a signal to head for the hills, perhaps running toward another dog they see, to the scent of a female in heat, or to the smell of food. Dogs who have run away from their owners have done so to the regret of the owners, compared to roaming dogs whose owners allowed unrestricted access to the outdoors right from the start.

Some dogs run away after accidentally jumping out of the car, then becoming frightened at the confusion and noise of a parking lot or road. These dogs often get hit by cars before the panicked owners can effectively call the pets back.

WHY YOUR DOG IS DOING THIS

Dogs who run away from their owners when let off the leash so primarily due to poor owner control. Whether neutered or not, a dog should always be trained to come when called, for safety's sake and to prevent the pet from becoming lost. Many owners take their dogs off-leash well before the dog is ready to be trusted with that level of freedom. Suddenly overwhelmed by hundreds of scents, sights, and sounds, young, poorly trained dogs take off to have fun, oblivious to their owners' protestations. This type of dog has very little respect for the owner's leadership skills, which, in this case, are nearly nonexistent.

Frightened dogs may also run away from their owners if off the leash and suddenly confronted with a frightening situation. If scared by fast-moving cars or by another dog, insecure dogs might head for the hills in panic. A normal response for a terrified animal, the "fight-or-flight" instinct kicks in, making such pets oblivious to owners' calls. By the time these dogs have calmed down, they are lost.

SOLUTION

The first step in stopping your dog from running away is having him or her neutered. Doing so (if you haven't already) will dramatically reduce the desire to seek out appropriate mates and confront other dogs.

To prevent your dog from running away from you while outside, be sure to start obedience training as soon as he is ten or twelve weeks old. You must establish leadership with him as early on as possible, as well as solid control under any circumstances. When trained properly, a respectful dog will want to come to you when called. It is only disrespectful, dominant, or untrained dogs who blatantly refuse to come when called. Dominant dogs consider the owners' protestations to take a backseat to their desires at the moment, which could include chasing a cat or another dog or begging food from some picnickers 100 yards away.

Before ever considering letting your dog off-leash outdoors, you need to have a rock-solid recall or *come* command thoroughly ingrained into your dog's head. Start when the dog is young and work the command in the home first, at the end of a six-foot leash. Clip the leash on his collar, then wait for a moment when his attentions are not on you. Then, while holding the end of the leash, crouch down and call the dog to you in a happy voice. Don't say, *"Come!"* in a commanding tone; instead, try saying, *"Bobo, come here!"* in a happy, fun tone. The dog will probably shoot over to you, whereupon you should give him a treat and lots of physical praise. If he doesn't immediately come to you, say, "No," and then repeat the command to come while gently pulling on the leash. If need be, use the leash to physically bring the dog over to you. The one abiding rule in teaching the recall to your dog is to never allow the dog the opportunity to ignore your command. You must always be able to get him to come to you, or else he will learn that you have no consistent control over him. By using gradually lengthening leads attached to the dog's collar, you guarantee that he has no choice but to eventually come to you. You can reel him in if need be. But he comes, every time, with no other choice.

Gradually lengthen the lead connected to your dog's collar until you can reliably get him to come to you from twenty feet away in the backyard. Don't work this in a park yet, as there will be too much distraction going on for your dog to concentrate. Always reward him with a treat and physical praise at this point. If he gets distracted, jerk on the lead, say, *"No!,"* and then call him again. Eventually he will come to you reliably while on the extended lead. Then take him back into the quiet home, place him at the end of a hallway, and call him to you, without the benefit of a leash. If you have done it right, he will shoot over to you happily. When he does, give him a treat and some hugs. After working this inside the home for a few days, take your dog out to a fenced-in yard. Call him happily; he should bolt over. If he doesn't, calmly walk over to him (do not rush over!), clip his leash on, then go back to using the twenty-foot lead.

You must get your dog to reliably come to you in the yard, off-leash, before ever taking him off-leash in a park.

While working this exercise, gradually reduce the amount of treats you use until your dog gets one only once in a while. This will actually improve his response time. Trainers have known this for a long time; sporadic rewards always motivate better than giving rewards after every trial, which becomes passé to the pet after a while. If you keep him guessing, he will work faster for you.

The recall or *come* command is the most important one to teach your dog, as it might save his life one day. If he jumps out of your car while in a busy parking lot, you can quickly call him over to you, praise him, then put him back in the car. To keep this from occurring, use a travel crate when transporting your dog in the car. This will prevent him from escaping and getting struck by a car or from running away in a panic.

To perfect the recall command with your dog, attend an obedience class with him, where the instructor can go over the fine points and give you expert advice that relates directly to your dog. Plus, the added distraction of all of the other dogs in the room will help you teach him that he must come to you despite the presence of other animals and persons.

SEPARATION ANXIETY

DESCRIPTION

Some dogs can and do suffer from separation anxiety when apart from their owners or from other pets in the home. The dog who suffers during times of separation can show destructive behavior and may vocalize excessively, to the point of disturbing neighbors. In addition, your lonely dog may redirect his anxiety into nervous grooming and overgroom himself to the point of causing hair loss or skin disorders. Many dogs suffering separation anxiety develop lick sores or chronic dermatitis. Lonely dogs might also lose much of their appetite and lose substantial amounts of weight. German shepherds and dalmatians are especially susceptible to this malady. Often the behavior becomes a problem for boarding kennels, responsible for anxious dog welfare while their owners are off on vacation. While being boarded, dogs suffering from separation anxiety often do not eat or drink at all and end up inflicting terrible lick sores on their front paws.

WHY YOUR DOG IS DOING THIS

Several causes might be at work in the dog suffering from separation anxiety. First, pets acquired well before their eighth week of life are much more likely to show signs of this problem, as they were not allowed to experience the full amount of socialization necessary to create a stable social mind-set. The time puppies spend with their mothers and littermates is vital to the formation of their social psyches; if taken from the litter before their eighth week, they may never become properly socialized and can develop an insecure persona. In addition, when a five- or six-week-old puppy goes home with a new owner, the pet tends to bond very closely to that person, so closely that the absence of that owner, even for a short period of time, can create great emotional stress for the dog. Bottle-fed orphans are particularly susceptible to the problem, as the owner becomes the surrogate mother, someone the dog cannot seem to be without for too long.

Some dogs who exhibit profound separation anxiety simply have hereditary predisposition toward the behavior. With these pets, the fear of isolation seems to have been programmed into their personalities. When this is the case, modifying the behavior becomes extremely difficult.

Dogs who rarely socialize outside of their own immediate families often have a hard time being apart from them, as they have no experience with other persons or dogs and only feel at ease around those they trust and love. Owners who work long hours and don't find time to socialize their pets often find that their canine friends simply can't handle strangers well. In addition, the large blocks of time hard-working owners stay away from the home eventually wreak havoc on many dogs, as they were never meant to live a life of complete isolation.

Dogs who suffer from *hypothyroidism*, or an underactive thyroid gland, often suffer separation anxiety as a symptom of the condition. German shepherds and dalmatians have a higher incidence of this disorder than do other breeds, perhaps explaining why they experience separation anxiety so much more often. These two breeds also tend to be somewhat high-strung and sensitive in nature, perhaps adding to the problem. German shepherds, known for their extraordinary devotion, often fare poorly when left alone.

Strays and rescued dogs tend to develop this disorder more often than others. They have led lives of unpredictable, unreliable camaraderie, bouncing from one owner to another or having to survive outside on their own. When adopted by a loving owner, shelter dogs and strays sometimes can't believe their good fortune and thus bond incredibly closely to their new master, so much so that they cannot bear to see him or her leave, for fear that it might be the last time they see him or her. This profound insecurity resembles closely a three-year-old child's reaction to being left at a day-care center for the very first time.

The absence of an owner is not the only factor that can trigger separation anxiety. The departure or death of another family pet (usually a dog but sometimes a cat) can also cause profound separation anxiety in the remaining dog, especially if they have been together for many years.

Owners who pamper and spoil their dogs inadvertently create pets who cannot cope well with being alone or being left in the care of someone else for a short time. Toy dogs often suffer separation anxiety quite badly, as they tend to be coddled and overprotected by their owners, who often treat their pets as if they were surrogate human babies. While enjoying the attention, these toy dogs develop a self-centered, egotistical attitude. When suddenly separated from the source of their egotism, however, they collapse emotionally, due to separation anxiety.

SOLUTION

Once a dog has exhibited symptoms of separation anxiety, it is difficult to modify the behavior. Techniques worth trying include having a friend or neighbor stop by the home once each day while you are gone to interact with the dog for at least a few minutes at a time and hiring a pet sitter to stop by two or three times each day. Doing so can help forestall some or all of the symptoms of the problem, particularly the destructive behavior, often evidenced by marred or ripped furniture, or failure of the dog's house-training habits.

You can also try making your dog's environment as exciting as possible by putting down numerous chews and toys, hiding treats around the home, and leaving a radio or television on while you are gone. Some owners will even purchase a pet video tape and play it for their dogs while they are gone. These videos, available at many pet stores, show cats, dogs, or other animals on the screen, in a size that appears most lifelike to your pet. The shapes and movements seen by him can often act as a great distraction, keeping him from worrying too much about being alone.

Here is another trick to try. Go to the electronics supply store and purchase a blank, thirty-second outgoing message cassette tape, the type you might use in an answering machine. These tapes are of the endless loop variety; if played in a normal cassette recorder, they will play whatever is recorded on them over and over again. Slip the tape into a cassette recorder and record yourself saying something like, *"Hi, Bobo; are you a good boy?"* After doing so, play the recording. You will find that the tape recorder will recycle the recording over and over again, as long as it is left on play. You can then play this tape in a cassette player while you are gone so that the dog will hear your voice every thirty seconds or so. Try leaving the player on in another room, with the door closed; this way, your dog will hear you behind the door and possibly think you are still home. For many dogs, this technique can be just the trick to minimize their anxieties.

When choosing a puppy or adult dog, be sure to select wisely. Always pick the puppy or adult dog who seems curious and confident, yet not overbearing. Never choose the shrinking violets in the corner just because you feel sorry for them. You might end up with an insecure, timid pet who can't stand to be without you. Also, never take puppies home before their eighth week, as this would interfere with the development of their social nature. Allowing puppies to interact with their mothers and littermates until the end of their eighth week will ensure they learn proper social etiquette and give them ample time to begin developing their own individual personalities. Without these factors present, puppies may develop antisocial tendencies and separation anxiety later in life.

Be sure to properly socialize your puppy or adult dog from the moment you bring him home. Get him used to other persons and allow him to visit the homes of friends as well, so that he will be comfortable with them should you need to go on a trip in the future. Walk him down busy streets, take him to municipal dog parks, and let other persons work his basic obedience. If he learns to obey people other than you, he will learn to trust them as well, making it easier for him to stay with them in case you need to travel for a week or two. Whatever you do, don't isolate your pet at home every day for hours upon hours. Remember that dogs are pack animals and were never designed to spend life alone.

If you adopt a stray or rescued dog, try not to spoil and

pamper him, even though he has had a rough life. Doing so will cause him to rely on you for everything, making it impossible for you to leave the home without his becoming a nervous wreck. Obedience-train your rescued dog or stray immediately to give him structure and to involve his mind.

When you leave the home, try not to make a big scene with your dog. Don't get down on the floor and have a long talk with him, telling him how much you will miss him. By doing so you will be creating an emotion-filled departure ritual that signals him of your imminent exit. Instead, five minutes before you leave begin ignoring the dog. Then just leave, without saying a word. Doing so will defuse the departure ritual and eventually help stop him from becoming anxious over you leaving. Also try leaving the home and coming back in a minute or so, randomly, so that the dog can no longer predict when you will be back. Stay away for a minute, five minutes, an hour, or a second. Mix it up, so he will never know. This way, you will create a slight sense of expectancy in his mind, perhaps enough to overcome his anxiety. When you do come home, try the same technique; ignore him for a few minutes, instead of making a big production over him. Then quietly pat him on the head and say, *"Hi, Bobo."* That's it. In this way, you will defuse the greeting ritual. Having an emotional greeting with your dog only serves to make future separations that much harder. Don't do it.

Do not spoil your dog! He is a dog, not a child. Don't treat him as if you gave birth to him. Treat him like a trusted canine, and he will be the better for it. A spoiled dog develops a false sense of importance and becomes dominant and pushy. In the end, though, his ego becomes inexorably tied to your presence; without you, he falls like a deck of cards. By setting rules and treating him like a dog you will help foster confidence, trust, and independence.

If your dog develops separation anxiety due to the death of another beloved pet, don't rush out to the shelter or breeder and get another, hoping that that will cure the problem. Instead, allow your remaining dog to grieve, just as you allow yourself to. Then, after a month or two, consider adopting or purchasing another dog, provided your pet isn't dog-aggressive. A puppy should be easily accepted and might help fill the emotional void for both of you. If adopting an adult dog, be sure to have your own pet meet the new dog on neutral turf before deciding, to be sure they get along.

SEXUAL PROBLEMS

DESCRIPTION

Several behavioral problems can arise out of your dog's expression of his or her sexuality. First and foremost is the risk of pregnancy and the specter of having to care for (and find homes for) several newborns. Next is having to deal with all of the behavioral problems associated with mating and courtship, including marking, spotting, fighting, and birthing. Regardless of what gender canine you have, most or all of these undesirable behaviors will eventually pop up, especially if your unneutered pet is allowed unrestricted access to the outdoors.

Once an unneutered male reaches seven to ten months of age, he will probably begin to exhibit behaviors related to his sexual desires. He will want to search out females in heat, raising the risk or injury or loss of the pet. He may also get into fights with other competing males, often requiring a trip to the veterinarian. In addition, he will mark his territory around (and even perhaps inside) your home.

An unneutered female will reach sexual maturity at about seven to ten months and will also immediately show sexually driven behaviors, including spotting from being in heat, and a desire to get outside and find a male. Though this is less common in females, she too may mark territory with urine, and she may experience changes in her elimination habits. If impregnated by a male, she will eventually search out a nesting area and give birth, after a gestation period of about sixty-three days. During the birthing period, she may become somewhat antisocial and protective of the puppies.

WHY YOUR DOG IS DOING THIS

The drive to mate is perhaps the strongest instinct in all of nature, taking a backseat to no other, except perhaps the hunger drive. Any unneutered dog therefore may exhibit any or all of the aforementioned behaviors, once past the age of seven months. Trying to modify the behaviors while still refusing to neuter the dog is a futile gesture; without neutering, you may have to put up with a damaged, odorous home or else just keep the pet outside in a pen all the time. Also, an unneutered male, if allowed unrestricted access to the outdoors, runs the risk of getting hit by a car in his attempts to find a female.

SOLUTION

The way to prevent any or all of the aforementioned sexually related behavior problems in your dog is to simply have the pet neutered before sexual maturity, usually by the sixth or seventh month. By doing so you will prevent damage to your home, possible injury to your dog, and the unnecessary birth of unwanted puppies, who will in all likelihood have to be euthanized for lack of good homes. Neutering will also increase the life span of your dog, by lowering the chances of uterine, ovarian, or testicular cancer and by preventing roaming, which often leads to death from car mishaps. Do yourself and your dog a favor, and choose neutering. Doing so will make life for both of you happier, less stressful, and safer.

SWIMMING, AVERSION TO

DESCRIPTION

Though normally instinctive swimmers, some dogs can have an initial fear of water or else develop a fear of it due to a bad experience. Dogs who are reluctant to go in the water may cautiously step in, then run back up on dry land. Or they may avoid the water entirely.

WHY YOUR DOG IS DOING THIS

Various reasons might explain why your dog is showing a fear of the water. She might have at some point been thrown in against her will or manhandled while swimming, causing her to swallow water and panic. Or her first experience might have been in an excessively cold lake or stream, the frigid temperature of the water causing her concern. Thin dogs especially can suffer from the cold water; sight hounds, with their thin skin and coats, tend not to enjoy cold water. A fast-running river may have taken your dog downcurrent for a bit, causing her to panic. Or she might have become sick from swallowing too much water. Some puppies, when taken to an ocean beach, can get salty water in their eyes, causing stinging. A young puppy might even become frightened of the surf crashing into the shore.

Some muscular, big-boned breeds such as the rottweiler, pit bull, bull mastiff, and mastiff have a very dense body, which often does not afford the dog much buoyancy. Because of this, heavy, compact dogs can become fatigued more rapidly, despite their strength, perhaps swallowing water and panicking. Obese dogs should also be watched carefully, as should dogs with thick, heavy coats (such as the komondor, Old English sheepdog, puli, and malamute), which can absorb pounds of water and make swimming nearly impossible.

SOLUTION

First and foremost, never force your dog into the water. Allow her to go in under her own steam, out of curiosity. With a puppy, try going into the water yourself, perhaps up to your ankles, and then encouraging her to follow you in. You can also use her favorite ball or waterproof toy as a lure to get her in with you. Be sure that the water isn't too deep or cold, and really praise her for even sticking one paw in. Avoid choosing a fast-moving river as her first experience, as this can leave a bad impression on her. You might even lose her to the current, if she is small enough or river fast enough.

If your dog loves to fetch, work it near the shoreline of a calm body of shallow water. Once she is really hyped to fetch, try tossing the ball in the water and see what happens. If she retrieves it, praise her lavishly. If she is a retriever, spaniel, or perhaps a Newfoundland, odds are she will leap into the water the first time she sees it, as these breeds were designed to love water.

If your dog already has a fear of the water, you will just need to be patient. Take her to a calm, shallow body of warm water and bring along a few other dogs who love to swim. When she sees them having fun in the water, odds are she will eventually want to join in. When she does, praise her. Then, after getting her out of the water, give her a treat. Just remember never to press the issue.

UNDERACTIVE BEHAVIOR

DESCRIPTION

Underactive dogs don't seem to move around as much as they once might have and may refrain from playing or interacting. They might show fluctuations in weight and might or might not be more vocal than usual. Dry coat and skin might develop. Underactive dogs may also sleep more than usual and be lethargic when awake. They might appear more impatient or irritable and could even show an exaggerated sensitivity to touch.

WHY YOUR DOG IS DOING THIS

Several factors could be causing your dog's underactive behavior. First, an uncommon condition called *hypothyroidism* could be developing. Caused by a severe reduction in the production of hormones by the dog's thyroid gland, the result is a slowdown in her metabolism. A hypothyroid condition may also cause your dog to gain weight. The dog might sleep more and develop coat and skin problems, particularly dry, brittle hair and itchy skin.

Advancing age will have a slowing effect on your dog's behavior as well. Old age slows her metabolism and causes her to sleep more. Aching joints may limit her ability to move. Her appetite could fluctuate, as could her weight, which often increases with age, due to the slowing metabolism.

Injury or illness can also be a major cause of underactive canine behavior. Dogs tend not to broadcast their aches and pains and instead choose to lay low and stay quiet. This stoic attitude often blinds us to the presence of a serious condition. Injured or sick dogs, in addition to being nearly inactive, will lose their appetite and be extremely sensitive to touch.

SOLUTION

The very first step in dealing with an underactive dog is a trip to the veterinarian. Once you are there, the doctor will be able to determine if your dog has an underactive thyroid gland or if illness or injury might be the culprit. If old age is the cause, the veterinarian will be able to determine that as well and also give advice on how to deal with it, including dietary changes to deal with a possible deficiency or rearrangement of the dog's environment to better suit her flagging physical capabilities (see "Old Age, Behavioral Problems Related To").

If the problem is being caused by an underactive thyroid gland, you will have to give your dog medication every day to counteract the deficiency (see "Pill Taking, Aversion To"). Once your dog is on the synthetic hormones, her activity levels and overall health will return to normal.

If the sluggish behavior is due to illness or injury, try to determine how it occurred. Is your dog allowed unrestricted access to the outdoors? If so, she might have contracted an illness from another dog or else been struck by a vehicle.

In addition, underactive behavior can be caused by depression. To that end, refer to the listing "Depression."

VETERINARIAN, AVERSION TO

DESCRIPTION

Most dogs do not savor going to the veterinarian for annual checkups. After all, being poked and prodded by a total stranger isn't anyone's idea of a fun afternoon. Your dog's temperature is taken, blood may be drawn, and his ears and mouth must be looked into. During all of this, some dogs simply won't sit still, sometimes causing the veterinarian and his or her assistants to have to immobilize the dog to facilitate the exam. As this may be the only contact your dog and the veterinarian ever experiences, you can begin to understand why the mere sight of the clinic might depress your dog.

Some fearful dogs will resist the probing and restraining and try to extricate themselves from the situation. When unsuccessful, some will reluctantly accede, while others will attempt to bite. Most dogs fall somewhere in between, causing veterinarians to earn their pay.

WHY YOUR DOG IS DOING THIS

Let's face it: from your dog's point of view, the veterinarian is a controlling bully. Your dog does not feel at all comfortable with a total stranger taking such physical liberties. When the veterinarian persists, your dog can begin to fear the situation. He cannot run away, though, so he may panic and try to fight his way to freedom, which usually fails, leaving him to surrender to the moment.

Dogs have good memories. If someone accidentally (or otherwise) hurts a dog, the pet might retain that memory forever and may never feel at ease around that person again. Such is the lot of the veterinarian. In trying to examine and treat the dog, he or she must create a humiliating and scary situation for the dog, who will retain the memory and resist the veterinarian's wishes, no matter how careful and gentle he or she is.

SOLUTION

We must try to make the veterinarian's life a bit easier. One way to do it is to handle our dogs each and every day, starting in early puppyhood. From the very first day you should regularly pick your dog up, examine his body, look into his ears and mouth, and check his coat and skin for parasites. Brush and comb him frequently, and give him a delicious treat as a reward after each handling or grooming session. By desensitizing him to examination from a very early age you will be making your veterinarian's job much easier. Doing so will help you keep your canine in the best shape possible.

If your dog already hates going to the veterinarian, there isn't much that can be done except to attempt to alter his opinion of the place. Try visiting the veterinarian's office every now and then for a "nonvisit." Take your dog in for a quick "hello" from the staff there, who can (if time allows) pet your dog and give him treats. You can even play with him right there in the office, provided there are no other animals in the reception area. Take his favorite ball with you and get him to fetch it for a minute. Praise and reward him, then leave with him. If the staff at the clinic is tolerant of your doing this, it will help to at least partially defuse the dog's fears of going there.

Some dogs become so fear-aggressive that they must be sedated in order to be examined. If this is the case with your pet, ask your veterinarian to prescribe a mild sedative that the dog can be given before the visit. Normally provided in pill form, the sedative will calm him down enough to allow the exam to take place.

PART THREE

The Ten Most Important Ways to Minimize Canine Behavioral Problems

This last section provides you with the ten most valuable measures you can take to ensure a trouble-free dog and a great pet/owner relationship. Meant to be fast and easy to read and reread, each of the ten "commandments" will be about a page or less in length. They will aid owners in preventing major and minor canine behavioral problems and help strengthen the bond between owner and pet. Take some time now to go over each one carefully, so you can begin applying them to your dog right away.

1. SCHEDULE A YEARLY VISIT TO YOUR VETERINARIAN

Every dog should make at least one trip to the veterinarian each year, not only to receive an overall examination but also to be administered the proper immunizations. In addition, this annual visit will allow your veterinarian to become as familiar as possible with your dog and permit him or her to compare your pet's appearance and behavior over time. Being able to do so is a valuable diagnostic tool for the doctor, who may be able to notice a change in behavior or appearance better than you, who might not notice subtle changes over time. Weight gain, for instance, often occurs too slowly for many owners to notice. To the veterinarian, however, the gain will be obvious.

If your dog is ill or injured, try to have as much information as possible available for the veterinarian. Be accurate with the symptoms or with the details of the accident, if your dog was hurt in some way.

Remember that of all the individuals involved in your dog's life, next to you the veterinarian is the most important. He or she may spot a serious medical problem before it has a chance to adversely affect your dog's health and behavior. The veterinarian can also give you sound advice on behavior and even on areas such as diet, breeding, training, and pet selection. Keeping in touch with your veterinarian is one of the best ways known to help minimize all manner of dog problems, so don't be shy!

2. ATTEND AN OBEDIENCE CLASS WITH YOUR DOG

As an absolute necessity for ensuring a good relationship with your dog, be sure to attend a six-to-eight-week-long obedience class with him, preferably while he is still a puppy and certainly before his first birthday. It will help establish for both of you just what fundamental rules should be in place and what a good dog/owner relationship is really all about. If purchasing or adopting an adult dog, however, don't fret; though a young animal is always more impressionable, a dog of any age can easily learn to behave in an acceptable fashion.

Both you and your dog will benefit tremendously from attending the class. He will learn how to behave properly and to also respect your position as leader of your pack. You will learn the subtleties of canine behavior and how important it is to always act in a dominant yet fair manner. In addition, both of you will learn how to properly socialize with the other dogs and persons in the class. He will also come to understand that obedience is a must, regardless of the situation at hand. Whether alone or among a group of dogs or people, your dog must always act in a responsible fashion. The instructor of the class will teach both of you how to do just that.

3. BE THE UNDENIABLE LEADER OF YOUR PACK

Always remember that your dog is a pack animal, genetically programmed to be part of a group and to obey the dominant member of the pack. If you do not provide him with fair, strong, consistent leadership, he will attempt to fill those leadership boots himself. If that happens, behavioral trouble can abound. Don't let it happen. Instead, do everything you can to show your dog who is in charge. This includes:

◆ Not allowing your dog to sleep in bed with you.
◆ Eating before he does.
◆ Never allowing your dog to mouth a human being.
◆ Never chasing your dog or playing excessively rough games with him.
◆ Going through doors before he does.
◆ Not allowing him to pull ahead of you while on the leash.
◆ Initiating and controlling as many interactions as possible.
◆ Being calm, fair, and confident.
◆ Protecting your dog from other animals or malicious persons when necessary.
◆ Never allowing your dog to get away with improper behavior.

If you stick to these basic leadership caveats your dog will learn to respect you as a leader and trust you implicitly. With this respect and trust will come a deep love and a tremendous desire to please. Be a good leader, and your dog will *want* to obey you.

4. NEVER HIT OR ABUSE YOUR DOG IN ANY WAY

Though this directive may sound obvious to all who read it, dog abuse remains one of the major causes of canine behavioral problems today. Smacking or kicking a dog in an effort to get him or her to stop some undesirable behavior will not only result in a permanent breakdown of the dog/owner relationship but can cause serious or fatal injury to the pet as well, whose body cannot possibly hold up to being struck by a human being.

More dogs are hurt or killed by human beings each year than by anything else. The tragedy of this statement is that we have a choice not to harm a smaller creature but often do nonetheless, out of either frustration, anger, or some hard-to-define sadistic rationale.

Dogs react poorly to verbal abuse as well. Yelling and screaming doesn't work well on dogs, who will become stressed at your tirade and in all likelihood exhibit additional behavior problems as a result. For us to scream at a dog is contrary to the very reasons we own one, namely, love and companionship. Instead of losing your temper, calm down and train your dog through the problem. Use your mind and your heart, instead of your foot or your lungs.

5. READ AS MANY BOOKS AND MAGAZINES ON DOG BEHAVIOR AS POSSIBLE

Knowledge of canine behavior and physiology changes and increases every day. As a dog owner, you should attempt to keep up with these changes as best you can for the sake of your pet. In addition, new products designed specifically with the dog in mind come onto the market every day; many might be of great value to you in your attempts to maintain a good relationship with your pooch.

Take a trip to your local bookstore and take a look at just how many dog-related books are offered. Topics range far and wide and include information on breeds, behavior, new trends, diet, medicine, toys, and a host of other important categories. You can learn what the experts have to say about your specific breed of dog, learn about a new breed, or even find out how to teach your dog tricks. With the popularity of dogs all over the world, available information on them has been increasing dramatically. To keep up, consider checking the bookshelves at your local bookstore.

For the most current information on dogs, check out the magazine racks. Today more than a half-dozen dog magazines are available for you to buy. Dog magazines will give you good information on all aspects of dog ownership and will also help put you in touch with breeders in your area, if you are in the market for a specific type of dog. Great articles on nutrition, health, and behavior will provide regular, invaluable additions to your dog "IQ."

By staying as informed as possible about all areas relating to dogs you will be better prepared to deal with any potential problems that might pop up in your own dog's life. Plus, you might learn something new about your favorite pooch!

6. WORK ON SOME ASPECT OF YOUR DOG'S OBEDIENCE, AT LEAST ONCE EACH DAY

Any behavior that isn't practiced regularly will eventually begin to fade away, be it piano playing or a proper "heel" by a dog. Because of this, you should keep your dog's obedience training up to snuff by working on it daily. Unfortunately, many owners take an obedience course with their dogs, then allow all the skills learned to languish, thinking that their pets will now be on "auto-pilot" for the rest of their lives. This just isn't the case. Remember that a dog has the reasoning capacity of a two-year-old human child. Have you ever known of a two-year-old who behaved perfectly, without need for guidance or discipline?

Choose some behavior, such as a sit-stay or a recall, and work on it for ten or fifteen minutes with your dog. Each day, choose a different behavior to improve or reinforce, as doing so will keep your dog's obedience honed, help maintain your status as leader, and give him something to think about and work toward besides eating and sleeping.

In addition, think about teaching your dog at least one new behavior every month. Make it simple. A trick, perhaps, such as *shake hands*, or *roll over*. Doing so will stimulate his mind and give both of you a sense of accomplishment.

Remember that dogs were bred to do some type of work; if you do not provide your pet with purpose, he will become restless and bored. Once that happens, bad behaviors are just around the corner. Working his obedience a little bit every day will prevent this from happening.

7. ALWAYS MAKE YOUR DOG EARN TREATS AND PRAISE

This short commandment is nevertheless an important one. Owners who give treats and praise to their dogs for no reason at all slowly but surely teach their pets to become pushy, controlling little beasts. The dogs learn to train their owners. By prompting you to give out a gratis treat or a pat on the head, your dog increases his status in the pack and begins to feel superior to you, who then wonder why your little pooch is no longer responding to commands. If your dog walks up to you while you are seated and shoves his head into your lap, he is saying, *Hey, pet me now.* You absentmindedly pat him on the head, not realizing that he has just trained you. Or, perhaps he nudges into you while you are preparing dinner, prompting you to give him a small piece of food. Every time you do, you tell your dog that he is running the show.

The simple solution is to ask your dog to perform some simple behavior in exchange for a treat or a hug. Ask him to *"sit"* or to *"shake"* before rewarding him. It's that simple. This teaches him that he must first respond to your command before being rewarded. You take the control back but still get to give him something he wants.

Avoid giving your dog something for nothing. Even a pat on the head can be preceded with a quick, *"Sit."* If you require this, he will continue to think of you as his benevolent master and not his lovable lackey.

8. KEEP YOUR DOG'S ENVIRONMENT AS INTERESTING AND SAFE AS POSSIBLE

Providing your dog with a fun, secure home life will go a long way in stimulating her mind, prolonging her life, and preventing bad behaviors. First, always have a number of fun toys available for her, including balls, veterinarian-approved chews, and wind-up or battery-powered animated toys. Old reliable toys such as crumpled balls of newspaper and Ping-Pong balls work well also. Be sure to initiate regular play sessions with her, to stimulate her mind and body and to help strengthen the bond between you both.

Provide your dog with a travel crate in the home to satisfy her occasional need for privacy. Leave a radio on every now and then, tuned to a talk station, to create the illusion of someone always being home, especially if your dog is prone to separation anxiety. Just be sure to keep it low, so as not to hurt your dog's excellent sense of hearing.

Remove all potentially toxic substances from your dog's domain, in order to preserve her health. Cleaners, solvents, motor oil, antifreeze, and any other poisonous materials should be safely stored away in a lockable cupboard. Be sure to remove any from your dog's environment toxic house or garden plants (see "Plant Eating"), which can cause severe illness or even death, if the dog is not treated promptly.

Socialize your dog as much as possible, to make her more accepting of strangers and to minimize barking, fear aggression, and jumping up. Having other persons and dogs in her life will make her a happier, better behaved pet and will help relieve boredom, often the precursor to problems. Also, try to take at least one dog-related class every two years or so, to keep her obedience fresh and to provide her with added stimuli, so important to good mental health.

9. NEUTER YOUR DOG

This one is really a no-brainer. If you are not a professional breeder, then you have no reason to avoid having your dog neutered by a competent veterinarian. Castration for the male and spaying for the female are both simple surgeries that cost little (usually about fifty dollars for castration and seventy-five dollars to eighty dollars for spaying) and can only improve the pet's demeanor. The drive to mate will be removed and the territorial instinct minimized. Plus, the chance of unwanted puppies being produced will be eliminated. Marking, fighting, roaming, spotting, and dominance issues will all be dramatically reduced or ended. You will be left with a more happy, personable pet, who will live longer and be statistically less likely to contract numerous forms of cancer.

Having the procedure done at around the sixth or seventh month of life will ensure that your dog has time to develop properly, both physically and mentally. Even dogs neutered before the fourth month make great pets, however, though they do tend to remain in a more "puppyish" state of mind all their lives.

10. LOVE YOUR DOG

We own dogs because of the companionship and love we feel for them and from them. A silent understanding should exist between owner and pet, one in which each knows the care and concern felt by the other. Both pet and owner feed off these feelings, making both feel wanted and secure. There is nothing better than developing and nurturing a partnership with a good dog.

Perhaps no piece of dog advice is more important than for you to love your pet unconditionally, despite whatever behavioral problems might pop up. When your dog feels true love coming from you, he will sense a stability and strength in the relationship, which will in turn calm him and help prevent behavioral problems from ever occurring. A well-adjusted, happy dog will be far less likely to act out than an abused, unloved animal. By openly caring for him you will do more to prevent problem behavior than all the pet books in the world could combined. And, besides, it'll make you a happier, better behaved person, too!

APPENDIXES

Appendix A

NATIONAL DOG ASSOCIATIONS AND ORGANIZATIONS

The American Kennel Club
5580 Centerview Drive, Suite 200
Raleigh, NC 27606-9767
(919) 233-3627

American Society for the Prevention of Cruelty to Animals
(ASPCA)
1755 Massachusetts Avenue NW, Suite 418
Washington, DC 20036
(202) 232-5020

Canadian Kennel Club
89 Skyway Avenue, Suite 100
Etobicoke, Ontario,
Canada M9W 6R4
(800) 250-8040

The Humane Society
2100 L Street NW
Washington, DC 20037
(202) 452-1100
(see also local listings)

The Owner Handler Association of America
RD1 Box 755

Millerstown, PA 17062
(717) 589-3098

The United Kennel Club, Inc.
100 East Kilgore Road.
Kalamazoo, MI 49001-5598
(616) 343-9020

Appendix B

MAGAZINES AND WEB SITES OF INTEREST

Magazines:

Dog and Kennel
Pet Business, Inc.
7-L Dundas Circle
Greensboro, NC 27407
(336) 292-4047
www.dogandkennel.com

Dog Fancy
PO Box 6050
Mission Viejo, CA 92690
(949) 855-8822
www.dogfancy.com

Dog World
500 North Dearborn Street, Suite 1100
Chicago, IL 60610
(312) 396-0600
www.dogworldmag.com

Web sites:

www.411pets.com
Breeder and services listings on the Web.

www.healthypets.com
A great site for health tips on your dog.

www.internetpets.com
A complete on-line pet store.

www.petfooddirect.com
A huge selection of premium pet foods and accessories.

www.petopia.com
A complete pet Web site.

www.pets.com
Everything you will ever need for your dog.

www.petsmart.com
Quality supplies and advice from this retail giant.

www.petstore.com
Good prices on food, toys, and whatever else you need.

SMP'S PET CARE BOOKS—
A PET OWNER'S BEST FRIEND . . .

Our books feature expert authors writing about today's most pressing pet care issues, from deciding to adopt to keeping a pet healthy.

ARE YOU THE PET FOR ME?
Choosing the Right Pet for Your Family
Mary Jane Checchi

WE'RE HAVING A KITTEN!
From the Big Decision Through the Crucial First Year
Eric Swanson

WE'RE HAVING A PUPPY!
From the Big Decision Through the Crucial First Year
Eric Swanson

AVAILABLE WHEREVER BOOKS ARE SOLD
FROM ST. MARTIN'S PAPERBACKS

The classic bestseller that began James
Herriot's extraordinary series...

All Creatures
Great and Small

JAMES HERRIOT

Let the world's most beloved animal doctor take
you along on his wonderful adventures through the
Yorkshire dales as he tends to its unforgettable
inhabitants—four-legged and otherwise.

"This warm, joyous and often hilarious first-person
chronicle of a young animal doctor...shines with
love of life."

—*The New York Times Book Review*

**AVAILABLE WHEREVER BOOKS ARE SOLD
FROM ST. MARTIN'S PAPERBACKS**